THE DATA INTEGRATION GUIDE

How to design, deliver, deploy, and sustain efficient data integration solutions in your information system

Ahmed Fessi

i

Table of Contents

Author's Note

Data is the new gold! But how can you access that gold mine?

After more than ten years of designing and delivering Data projects, specifically Data Integration ones, in various industries and locations with the main objective of unlocking Data potential, I came to realize that highly complex projects would have been much easier to conduct if they came with a comprehensive toolkit.

Complexity lies in every step: communicating with business stakeholders and gaining their buy-in, choosing the right solution, designing its architecture, finding the suitable approach for its integration into the global information system, delivering the project, defining viable and efficient patterns, choosing the right paradigms, as well as defining an efficient operations model.

This book aims to guide you through this journey, providing you with a complete toolkit that will save you a lot of time and effort to better scope, architect, deliver, and maintain Data Integration projects that provide you access to limitless data capabilities.

I hope you find the content as practical and tangible as I meant it to be!

The Data Integration Guide

CHAPTER ONE
Data Integration

Introduction

The Moore's law suggests that the processing power doubles every 18 months,

The Butter's law suggests the amount of data communicated through a single optical fiber doubles every 9 months,

The Kryder's law suggests that the amount of data stored per square centimeter of a hard drive will double every 13 months,

In 2022, we exchange, in 60 seconds, 200.000+ emails, and we perform four million searches,

The fact is that we have never created and exchanged volumes of data as we are doing today, and this is continuing to grow, not linearly, but exponentially.

This growth is accelerated by new needs and usages and a growing number of devices like servers, smartphones, or IoT (Internet of Things) devices, that are generating and consuming data, and backed by an underlying technology stack on data storage and data transfer that are becoming larger, faster, and more reliable.

This requires new approaches in data management and in managing data exchanges between systems.

On top of this technological trend, companies and organizations worldwide are looking at how Data can help them solve their business challenges and make relevant and efficient use of this new gold mine.

To achieve such an objective, we need to ensure proper data governance overall. Especially with the growing volume and evolving needs, data exchange and data integration have become key areas for controlling end-to-end data flows, but they may also raise doubts and risks about data confidentiality, security, and compliance.

In this book you will find a complete guide on how to define, build and maintain your data integration capabilities so that they can help you reach intended business outcomes.

What is Data Integration?

Before defining Data Integration, let's define Data and Integration.

Data is - un-interpreted - information that can be processed by computers.

It must be interpreted to become "information" and hence intelligible.

And what is Integration? According to Cambridge Dictionary, Integration is *"the action or process of combining two or more things in an effective way"*.

We can then derive the definition of Data Integration as the action of combining data to derive meaningful information and business value.

Data Integration in its more technical definition is the action of exchanging data between systems to respond to business use cases.

Data is produced by the systems, generally referred to as "source" systems or "producers". In order to get the data from those source systems, we can leverage a Data Integration Layer that connects to data sources and combines data to serve a business purpose.

The main objective is to support business processes by providing users (customers, business partners, business stakeholders, regulation authorities …) and systems with the right information at the right time.

An Example

To illustrate with real life examples and make this guide practical, many examples will be presented to help provide situations of usage of Data Integration from various industries.

We will consider 3 hypothetical companies: Best Bank which is an imaginary retail bank, Happy Tel which is an imaginary telecommunication operator and Smart Electronics which is an imaginary manufacturer of electronic goods. Any similarity to existing companies' names is totally coincidental, and those imaginary companies are only here to serve as examples of the notions and concepts presented in this guide.

Data Integration in Banking domain

Finance and Banking are big consumers of Data Integration, be it in retail banking, investment banking or all finance domains globally.

Data Integration is used daily to get currency rates, stock prices, or support high frequency trading, but it is also used to serve retail banking customers through mobile applications and web portals.

Let's assume you are a customer of Best Bank and you use your bank's mobile application. As a simple use case, you will need to access your account balance as well as the list of your last operations.

Actually, the mobile application you are using is leveraging a Data Integration layer that connects to your bank system with the objective to provide you as a customer with the right information (Balance) at the right time (Up-to-date information).

Data Integration in Telecommunications Industry

Telecommunications, with new emerging usages, have an increasing need for Data Integration, around every aspect of the telecommunications' value chain.

Data Integration can support provisioning new services, subscription processes, providing real time usage information to customers, selfcare portals and mobile applications.

Let's assume you are a customer at Happy Tel, a mobile operator, and you use the Happy Tel mobile application to subscribe to a new music service.

The operator mobile application will route your request to the operator systems and then to the network to provision the service. Once done, you will receive a confirmation that you have successfully subscribed to the new service.

All those actions: subscribing, provisioning and notification of fulfillment are enabled through Data Integration. In this case, Data Integration serves to provide you as a customer with the right information (confirmation or acknowledgment) at the right time (Up-to-date information) so you can start using the service.

Data Integration in Manufacturing

In Manufacturing, Data Integration has wide usages as well. It empowers the end-to-end supply chain as well as the manufacturer operations. It helps manufacturers support their processes and operations around the globe through real time ordering and invoicing, parcel tracking, inventory level follow-up as well as efficiency tracking and reporting.

Let's assume that Smart Electronics is a manufacturer of electronic goods. It sources electronic parts around the globe.

Smart Electronics wants to anticipate delays on its global supply chain. Using Data Integration, Smart Electronics will be able to get up-to-date information on the status of their last capacitors shipment sent by their Japanese supplier.

In this example, Data Integration is providing Smart Electronics with the right information (Status of Shipment) at the right time (Up-to-date information).

Let's Sum up!

Data Integration is about combining Data to derive meaningful information and ultimately business value.

Data Integration should be leveraged to help businesses achieve their goals by facilitating the data exchange required to efficiently fulfill business processes.

Data Integration is more than just a technical layer that transports data from one system to another; it is a building block that assists all sorts of businesses in meeting their goals.

CHAPTER TWO
Benefits & Business Value

Introduction

For many years, Information systems and IT have been viewed globally as a cost center in many enterprises and sectors. The financial view, which shows that a lot of cash is being consumed by IT, is always a challenge and difficult to explain from a business value perspective, and Data Integration might not break that "curse" unless it is clearly positioned as a business enabler.

Explaining the value behind investments in Data Integration is not an easy task, especially when it requires building a complete business case or an "ROI" (Return on Investment) validation.

The objective of this chapter is to help materialize and show tangible benefits of Data Integration investments.

Improving Customer Journey

Customers' expectations from goods and services providers have been continuously growing. What customers accepted 5 or 10 years ago, might no longer be acceptable today. Some usages have become quite natural, backed by strong data integration capabilities!

Today, it is becoming very natural to check if the new TV set you want to buy is available or not at your preferred retailer's nearest point of sale, and it is also very natural to know your real-time mobile plan usage without having to wait until the end of the month invoice arrives in your mailbox.

The examples are countless, but in a nutshell, Data Integration has enabled a much better customer journey by providing real-time information, and more reliable goods and services delivery overall.

Every business can seek new ways of improving the customer journey, which is crucial in supporting revenue growth, and Data Integration will assist in a variety of ways, such as offering better knowledge of your customers and their purchasing behaviors, delivering better service, providing more personalized customer care, or deploying loyalty programs. Data Integration should be regarded as an enabler, providing you with a powerful tool to help improve the overall customer journey and customer experience.

To illustrate with an example from the banking domain, let's suppose that Best Bank is receiving more and more complaints about operations performed using customer credit cards after they have been lost or stolen, especially if the customer was unaware that they had lost their card.

Best Bank can launch a new service that sends real-time notifications via its Data Integration Layer to its customers the moment their credit card is used. This way, they get alerted when the credit card is subject to illegitimate use. Overall, this improves the service they deliver to their customers by providing them with reliable, actionable, real-time information.

Improving the customer journey and experience can be accomplished in a variety of ways, with data integration providing strong support, for example, through offering a better experience with reliable information delivered on time, driving customer retention via improved customer service, or enhancing incident resolution times.

Reducing Time to Market

Time to Market is a key performance indicator for many businesses. It can be defined as the period required by a business between validating a new business idea (new product launch, new commercial action, new service, new loyalty program, etc.) and its effective launch.

Reducing time to market helps businesses become more agile and responsive to market challenges. Businesses that went through major crises like the subprime mortgage crisis in 2007-2008 or the Covid crisis in 2020-2021-2022, have learned, sometimes the hard way, the importance of having a very efficient time to market to be able to adapt to such situations. This is especially true for businesses who operate in competitive environments, where quick market responses are needed to maintain market shares in the face of fast-moving competition.

In such context, you can count on Data Integration as an enabler for actions requiring reduced time to market.

As an example, let's presume that Happy Tel wants to launch a new VOD (Video on Demand) service. The operator's customers will be able to access the VOD service directly through their mobile applications. As the mobile application is connected to a Data Integration Layer to get the list of available services, there is no need to release a new version of the application; instead, the existing ecosystem and data integration layer can be reused to support the quick launch of the new service, as well as future services.

In this case, the operator will only focus on the "back-end", ensuring that the core solution supporting the service is well-established, and will benefit from existing data integration services (like those used by mobile applications, but also self-care web portals, for example) to accelerate and quickly deliver new services to customers.

Cost Avoidance and Optimization

For their operations, businesses incur various costs, some of which may be avoided or optimized.

Data Integration can come to rescue by providing multiple use cases that help optimize costs.

First, it can help in "cost avoidance" scenarios, in particular regulation ones. In recent years, Electronic Invoicing (or E-Invoicing) has been heavily regulated to ensure proper and timely information transmission between business partners and regulation authorities (generally, tax authorities). Standardized formats have been published like FacturaE in Spain, Finvoice in Finland, ZUGFeRD in Germany or FatturaPA in Italy. In many cases, data integration will be the solution put in place to comply with those formats and to help organizations send their invoices in compliance with local laws and regulations. Failure to do so will cause expensive penalties generally.

Second, it aids in existing cost optimization by reducing inefficiencies in various business processes. Let's take the example of Smart Electronics. Smart Electronics needs to on-board a new supplier on their supply chain in order to source new microchips for their new product. On-boarding would generally include developing the whole connectivity channel and protocols with the new supplier; however, with the Data Integration Layer, the new supplier will reuse already existing processes for a quicker on-boarding, and thus reducing the cost, and eventually lead times.

Benefits from the Information System Perspective

Data Integration can be leveraged to "organize" and "urbanize" your information system. It will assist you in aligning your information system investments with your organization strategy, in the sense that it will help prepare your information system to offer better service, improve customer journey, and optimize costs.

From Information System perspective, deploying an enterprise-wide Data Integration solution, will bring various benefits:

- ✓ *Interoperability* will be assured between the applications composing your information system. Business applications are generally compared to data silos, where each business application generates and operates its own data, but independently from the rest of the systems, or by some basic batch or manual integration. Deploying a Data Integration solution will help simplify integrating applications and data exchange.

✓ *Reusability*: the connectors and data flows that will be built can be reused multiple times. Indeed, if you implement a connector, from your data integration layer to get customer information from your CRM (Customer Relationship Management) tool, for example, that connector can be reused by the billing or the ERP (Enterprise Resource Planning) tools at no further expense.

✓ *Reducing Time To Data*: Imagine you're in your workplace, and you ask your colleagues sitting nearby what the company's revenues were yesterday in a given geography; how many will be able to answer the question, and how long will they take? It's a typical exercise to materialize how sometimes it can be complex to acquire access to the right information, timely. Data Integration will support such use cases in ensuring data is provided to the right applications, systems, or stakeholders at the right time. Note that reducing time to data is directly correlated to key benefits like reducing time to market, optimizing decision cycles, and improving customer journey.

✓ *Data Integrity and Quality:* Data Integration is meant to automate integration within the information system. You might be surprised to know that today, a lot of data is still transferred manually, sometimes for critical business processes like customer delivery or financial statement elaboration. Such manual data manipulation can cause a degraded data quality due to errors and omissions that can occur naturally when a human being is transferring data across Excel sheets. Data Integration ensures data integrity (meaning, the data is not altered during its transfer), and in turn, data quality at the target.

✓ *Data Confidentiality & Security*: Depending on the data transiting in your information system, you might need to deal with various data confidentiality and security constraints. Confidentiality should apply to data that is sensitive for your organization or as per local regulations. For example, personal data, whether for your customers or employees, should be exchanged with respect to such constraints, so that emails, names, and other personal data are not visible to non-authorized personnel. Data related to the design of new products or sensitive financial information should be also exchanged with confidentiality constraints in mind. Data Integration Layer can help you maintain such confidentiality by ensuring that data is not manually manipulated and not visible to all employees. Furthermore, it helps enhance security by encrypting data while it is being transferred and protecting against man-in-the-middle breaches.

✓ *Scalability*: Having a dedicated Data Integration layer can help benefit from scalability. Indeed, you can adapt your underlying infrastructure sizing to the volumes and performance constraints you have by increasing available resources, like processing power and memory to adjust to an increasing volume of calculations or data. This adjustment can be permanent or temporary. New scalable architecture can allow you to automatically scale up or scale down your technical architecture to guarantee a smooth execution of your data integration processes.

CHAPTER THREE
Terminology, Main Concepts & Features

Terminology

A **Data Integration Layer** is an application (or a set of applications) that can integrate multiple applications,

A **Back-End** is an application that provides the data (also referred to as provider, producer, or source system).

A **Connector** is a software component that connects and gets the data from the back-end system. It provides the technical capability to connect to the source system.

A **Front-End** is an application that consumes the data (also referred to as consumer or target system), and in some cases, it may also trigger actions on the back-end (set attributes, create new data records ...)

An **Orchestration** is a complete end-to-end process in which a Front-End calls the Data Integration Layer, which orchestrates one or multiple calls to one or multiple Back-Ends.

The following diagram gives a view on the defined terms:

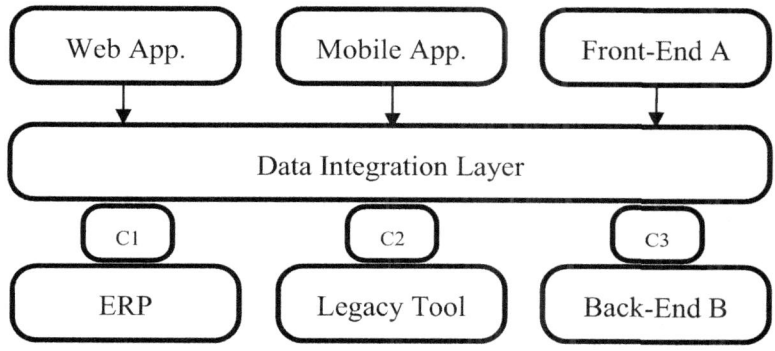

Figure 1: A simple representation of a data integration use case

In the previous diagram:

The Web Application, the Mobile Application, the Front-End A are Front-Ends.

The ERP, the Legacy Tool, and the Back-End B, are Back-Ends.

C1, C2 and C3 are connectors, providing connectivity capabilities respectively to the ERP, the legacy tool, and the Back-End B.

An example of Orchestration can be a process on which the mobile application calls the Data Integration Layer, that will orchestrate a call to the ERP and the Back-End B to obtain the data needed for the process.

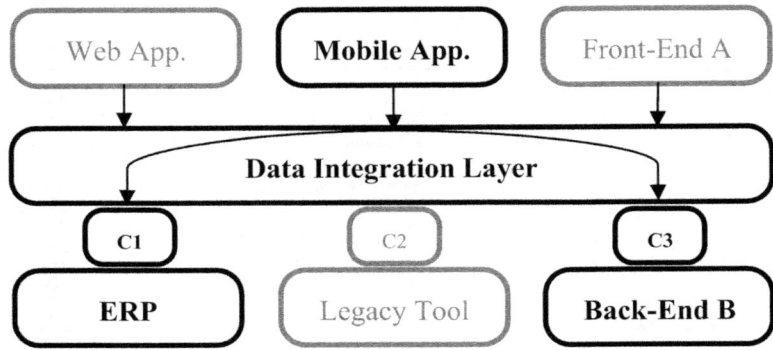

Figure 2: An Orchestration generic example

For a more tangible example, let's consider this diagram for a use case at Best Bank

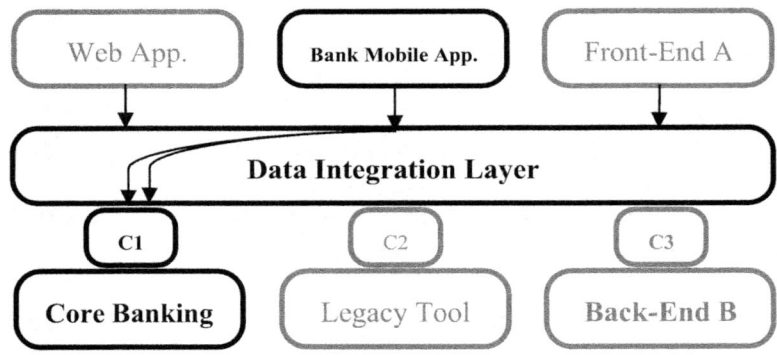

Figure 3: Example of Orchestration - Best Bank

In this example, the Back-End is the Core Banking software, the Front-End is the bank Mobile Application, and the use case implements an Orchestration, where the Mobile Application requests customer Balance and the list of Last Operations from the Data Integration Layer. The Data Integration Layer orchestrates 2 calls to the Back-End, the first to get balance and the second to get the list of operations.

Integrating Disparate Systems

Unless your information system was built in the last couple of years, starting from a greenfield, you will certainly have a fairly diverse set of applications and technologies. Some of your applications may support a given protocol (for example, SOAP web services), whereas others may not, and might only provide direct Database connectivity.

Moreover, you might have applications on your data center, some others may be hosted on the cloud, whether private or public. To integrate with such a wide range of cases, the Data Integration Layer will provide you with the necessary tooling to manage protocol translation and inter-zone (for example, on-premise to cloud) integrations.

Provide a Connectivity Layer via Connectors

Data Integration solutions come with a "toolbox", sometimes called Palette, Connectors Library, or Adapters Library.

It offers you a number of ways to connect to your applications through the connectors.

A connector represents the technical link between the data integration layer and back-end systems and more broadly, the applications you want to integrate through your Data Integration Layer.

Examples of Connectors include standard connectors to SaaS (Software as a Service) providers such as Salesforce or ServiceNow, standard webservices connectors for REST or SOAP, Database connectors both relational and NoSQL, or connectors to specific applications like ERPs.

Provide a Business Process Layer via Orchestration

The Data Integration Layer will enable the modeling and execution of business processes, which are sets of activities that result in a business outcome.

Following is an example of a simple business process for a new loan request submission from Best Bank.

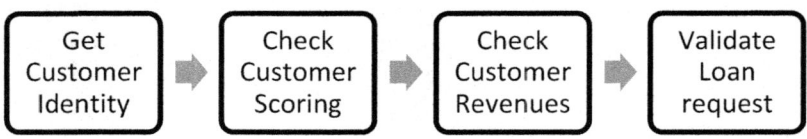

The Data Integration Layer will operate this multi-step process in a way to execute, step by step, each activity on the target system and produce the expected business outcome: submitting a valid loan request.

Provide Common Integration Services

The data integration layer generally comes with foundational components that will provide:

- ✓ Common Errors and Exception Handling framework, to help manage functional and technical errors, and specify how the system should react to errors. For instance, in case of timeout error while calling a back-end system, proceed with a retry.
- ✓ Logging framework, to provide comprehensive logging mechanisms with different levels of logging, that can be used by operations teams to monitor and supervise the data integration layer, as well as to help identify root causes in the event of a major service disruption or other incidents.
- ✓ Notifications, which may be triggered on specific events, such as generating an alert email in case of critical error or if a threshold on a critical metric is reached, like 95% CPU consumption.
- ✓ Supervision and operational reporting, comprising metrics and KPI on runtime such as response and execution time, resource (RAM, CPU, Disk...) consumption.

Support Service Composition and Modular Architecture

Service composition is a key feature in Data Integration tools that gives the possibility to combine multiple components in order to create new services.

The created components (or modules) can be reused to build other services in continuation.

Let's have a look to the two following different business processes from Best Bank.

Process A: Submit a Loan Request:

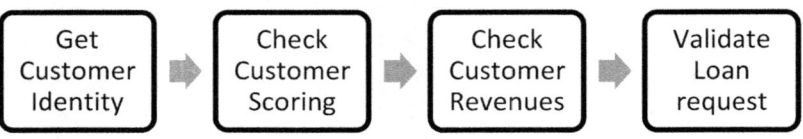

Process B: Submit a Credit Card Request:

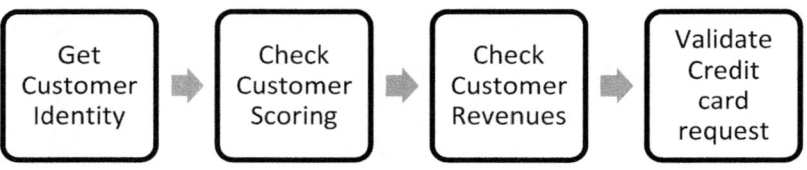

Both processes are comprised of multiple steps (or modules or sub processes). The first three steps are the same. Thus, the "Get Customer Identity" step (or module, or sub process) should be developed only once and reused. This reusability simplifies the architecture, the build, and the run management of your solution by applying modular architecture best practices.

The ability to combine the various steps to reach the desired business process model is made possible thanks to the service composition feature, which allows you to break any automatable business process down into smaller or granular modules that, when combined together, will achieve the desired business outcome.

To go further, we can also have a nested modularity, represented in the following example.

Process A: Submit a Loan Request:

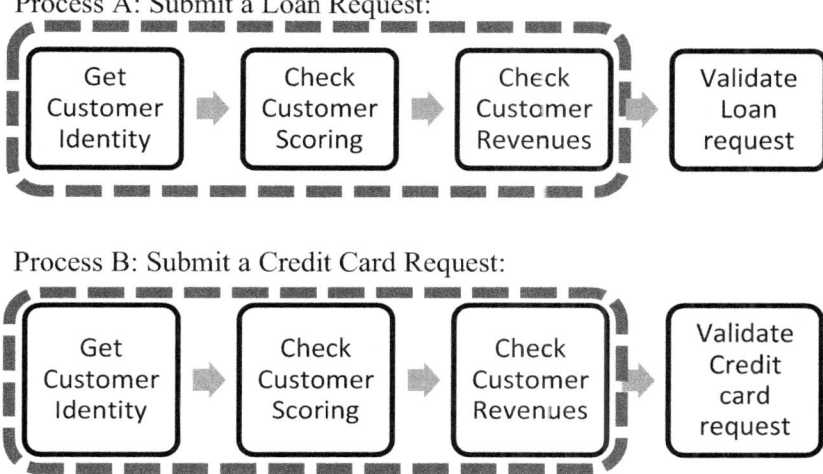

Process B: Submit a Credit Card Request:

The first three steps shared by both processes A and B can be grouped into one single module (group), that we can call "Get Customer Info" and that will be a combination of the first three steps.

> *"Service composition provides a multi-step business processes modeling capability to encompass calls to multiple back-end systems on the same transaction or call flow"*

Support Conditional Transitions

The Data Integration Layer provides you with multiple control and modeling options, including conditional transitions.

Conditional transitions are used in multi-step processes to adjust process behavior based on a comparison or test result.

The following example from Best Bank shows a simple conditional transition based on yearly revenue value, for instance, based on which a subscription package will be applied to the customer.

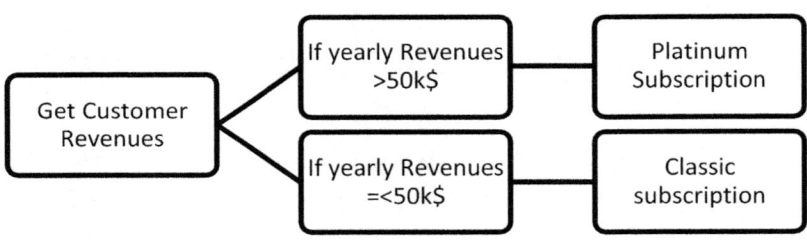

Support "Looping"

The Data Integration layer provides loop control as well.

You can, for example, implement a loop over an activity or a set of activities with "stop condition", like implementing a Retry mechanism: if the back-end application is generating a timeout, the Data Integration Layer will make a retry until it responds, or the process will fail after (x) retries.

Support Scheduling

Within the Data Integration Layer, you can define a scheduled process with configurable "wake-up" time.

This is very useful while implementing ETL (Extract, Transform, Load) processes. At a given pre-configured wake-up time, the defined process will be launched and executed without any manual intervention.

For example, Smart Electronics will execute a nightly process that will run every day at 00:05am to check the status of all parcels with shipping companies and raise alerts for late ones.

Hint: It is very common to schedule such processes on "off-peak" hours, meaning when the information system is not overloaded with heavy daily transactions, so that processes can run smoothly and without impacting on-going traffic on the Data Integration Layer.

Support Wait/Sleep Controls

The Wait (or Sleep) control allows performing a temporary configurable suspension of the running call flow.

For example, to avoid overloading target systems with heavy traffic, you can implement a 2 second "wait" between 2 consecutive retries in a retry process.

Throttling

Throttling control specifies a maximum number of calls per second limit (or another limit metric) for a certain activity, such as calling an external API or Web service.

Throttling prevents the system from crashing in case of a large number of concurrent requests, like DoS (Denial of Service) attacks.

It may, however, result in a latency and long waiting times, so it should be thoroughly designed and tested.

For example, Smart Electronics should limit their call to track their parcels with their logistics partner in order to comply with their limits. Such limits are generally communicated by the provider.

The following is an example from DHL website – API Developer Portal:

RATE LIMITS

Rate limits protect the DHL infrastructure from suspicious requests that exceed defined thresholds.

The table below details the main request limits:

Service Level	Maximum calls per second	Maximum calls per day
Starter	1	250
Standard	2	1000

Such a situation (throttling) should be considered whether your Data Integration Layer will be initiating the call, and the conditions are set by one of your backends, or in case your Data Integration Layer is acting as a provider of an API, for example, and needs to limit the number of calls it will receive.

Multicast Support

Depending on the chosen Data Integration Layer and its capabilities, it might be able to support Multicast. Multicast is a capability to propagate an information (notification, message or alert for example) to multiple endpoints in parallel.

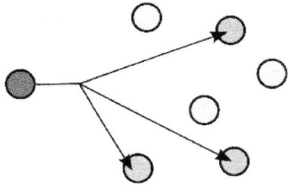

Data Transformation

Data transformation is a key feature in Data Integration that helps convert data from one format to another.

This feature aids in "translating" data between systems, so each system can ingest, use, or interpret it as per its defined business rules and data model.

Data transformation can vary in complexity. For simplification purposes, we will classify those transformations in three levels: Basic, Intermediate and Complex, and each of them will be presented in detail in the following sections of this chapter.

From an architecture standpoint, the Data Integration Layer should manage data transformation between integrated systems or applications. The Data Integration's role is to ensure that each system can use the data in its own data model and data format, and all transformation efforts should be "pushed" to the Data Integration Layer. This avoids putting such technical complexity on business applications and assures that the Data Integration Layer is used pragmatically, as it generally comes with out-of-the-box features supporting transformation between multiple data formats and allowing data model mapping with native tooling.

Basic Data Transformation

Basic Data Transformation encompasses simple operations that directly and simply convert Data Format A to Data Format B. This includes:

Data Type Conversions: such as converting float numbers to integers or vice versa. For example, converting 3.0 (float number) to 3 (integer)

Simple String Operations: Strings are the representation of a sequence of characters. Simple operations on strings, such as extracting the first n characters or last m characters are considered Basic Data Transformation and can be handled by the Data Integration Layer. For instance, removing the first three characters from the string "DATA" will provide "DAT" as a result. Such operations can be referred to as "substring" (extracting a subset of characters from the string).

Simple Calculations: Basic Data Transformations also include simple calculations like sums or products of 2 or more values. As an example, the sum of the series of integers 3, 5, 12 will give 20 as a result of this basic data transformation.

Date Format Conversions: If you have already manipulated data, you certainly know how hard it can be to manage different dates' formats: The US and European formats, for example, have most likely given you a headache. Date Format Conversions are important for bringing all of the dates in various data sets into the one common format you want to use, typically changing a date format in dd-mm-yyyy to mm/dd/yyyy (d refers to the day, m refers to the month, and y to the year. The number of repeated characters refers to the representation of the number on how many characters: yyyy means year in 4 digits, for example, and - or / refers to the "separator" to be used). As an example, applying the previous rule to 25-11-2022 gives 11/25/2022 as a result.

Intermediate Data Transformation

Intermediate Data Transformation covers Data Transformation operations of medium complexity. It is generally multi-step or set operations. This involves:

Lookup Operations: Lookup operations provide for a given 'key', a corresponding 'value'. For example, a Data Integration layer might provide a service that gives the country name, when given a country ISO code.

Country ISO Code	Country Name
AUS	Australia
BEL	Belarus
CYP	Cyprus
DEN	Denmark
FRA	France
TUN	Tunisia
...	...

So, let's assume that the Data Integration Layer receives a request to send back the corresponding Country Name of the country ISO Code "CYP": It will return "Cyprus".

Such lookup tables are also known as "Mapping" tables, as "Transcoding" tables or as "Cross reference" tables (can be abbreviated as "X-ref" tables). In a more direct manner, it's simply a list of key/value on which a value is returned for a given key.

When designing your Data Integration layer, there are some architecture choices that need to be made to define the pattern by which such an operation can be leveraged. There are many options available:

- *Native*: To have within your Data Integration layer the native possibility to define a lookup table. Some tools allow it through the tool designer, where you can enter the key values manually or upload them through a CSV or Excel file.
- *Database*: To have lookup tables in a Database coupled with your Data Integration Layer: while a Data Integration layer is generally a stateless, non-persistent tool, we may choose to back it up with a database to help store some configurations, read some reference data, store some logs, etc. This database can be leveraged to store the Lookup table, and each time the Data Integration layer receives a request, it will call the Database (as a local Backend) to get the related mapping.
- *Backend*: If the mapping can be provided by another application, it is also possible to get it dynamically. This is typically the case if you use a Master Data Management system to store and manage all your mappings. One caution with this design: each time you receive a request, you will make a call to the Backend system, which might create a certain load on the backend, but also create latency for your Data Integration Layer to provide the response.

- *Caching*: Caching can be a variant of the last two options: using a dedicated database or calling the backend: some Data Integration tools have a native "caching" feature that you can activate, where it gets the data only once in a given timeframe (for example, once per day) and store it in a cached mechanism within the Data Integration Layer. In this way, you avoid making multiple calls to the database or backend, and thus, removing the high load risk, as well as the latency. However, you risk using outdated data, as your cache might still have the old version when the data is updated.

Aggregations, series and sets operations: These are operations that apply to a set of values. They aim at providing either a feature of the whole data set (Average, Count, Maximum, Sum…) or to compute a specific representation of the data set (Sorted Data Set, Subset extraction based on a filtering option…).

Here are some examples of such operations. They are generally built-in functions within data integration layers.

- *Arithmetic Mean (Average) of a series number*: This applies the following mathematic formula:
  M is the average (arithmetic mean) of the x_i

$$M = \frac{1}{n} \sum_{i=0}^{n} x_i$$

- *Maximum or Minimum*: this helps to compute the maximum or minimum for a given set of numbers.

- *Median*: the median is the value separating the higher and lower sets of a data set. For example, 5 is the median of the following data set [7,4,2,5,10] (5 is bigger than 2 and 4, and is lower than 7 and 10).
- *Statistics and aggregation operations*: Depending on your needs, many other operations might be built-in or developed as customization. Statistics related operations are very useful if you are supplying a data set to an Analytics tool or a Data Science tool. However, there is one caution: The Data Integration tool should only support data transformation operations, however, it should not replace the business logic layer, which should be within the business applications or analytics layer.
- *Sorting*: For a given data set, sorting will provide you with the same data set but in a different order. Sorting can be done for both Numbers and Strings (set of characters). Here is an example of sorting in "Lexicographical" order: Lexicographical order means "like they would have been sorted in the dictionary".

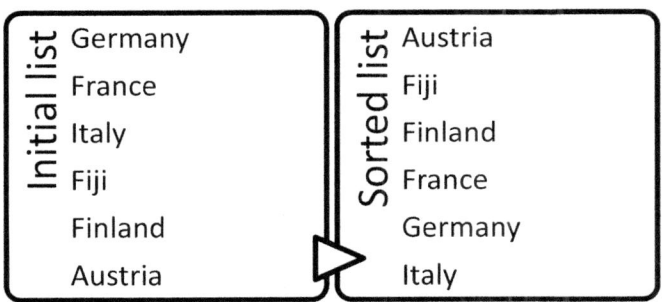

- *Curation*: curation operations apply to a set of data to make it usable by target applications. Typically, it can cover removal of all *NULL* values from a data set that will be used for a Data Science use case, or it can also apply some filtering or exclusion criteria to a data set. The result of a curation action is generally a (curated) subset of data that meets the criteria required by the target application.

Deterministic Matching: this operation looks for exact matching between two data sets or data objects. This is especially useful when a data integration layer is participating in a data reconciliation process, for example, identifying duplicates. Let's take a look at an example from Smart Electronics to identify duplicate checks in the list of suppliers. Two suppliers are considered the same if they have the same Duns & Bradstreet (D&B) unique code. The numbers used in the example are merely for illustration purposes.

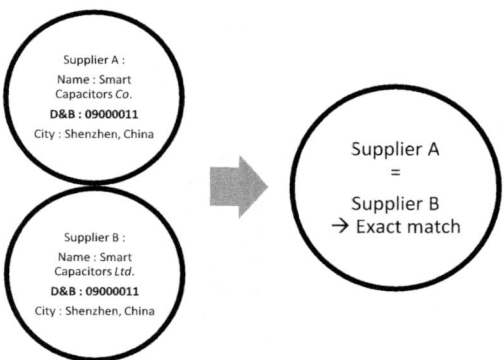

Complex Data Transformation

Complex Data Transformation is needed when Basic and Intermediate Data Transformation mechanisms are not sufficient, and the implementation requires a more sophisticated set of data transformation operations.

Probabilistic Matching: this operation uses algorithms and statistical methods to identify patterns or similarity probability in order to match data sets or records. Multiple algorithms and statistical methods support probabilistic matching and can be employed along with your data integration layer.

Fuzzy search is one good example of Probabilistic matching. Let's assume Bob is looking for information on how to subscribe to the new VOD (Video On Demand) service on Happy Tel Website's Frequently Asked Questions section. In the search field, he writes "How to active Video service", the website responds, via the integration layer he is connected to: Did you mean "How to activate VOD service on your mobile?"

Many algorithms can support such operations, and some might be built-in as an out-of-the-box feature within the data integration layer, or developed through custom development.

The Levenshtein distance computing algorithm, for example, can give you the "distance" between two strings, and thus an idea on how "close" the entry you have is to another reference string.

Other algorithms, such as Soundex or Metaphone are phonetic-based and may match strings like "Robert" to "Rupert" for example.

XSLT: XSLT stands for Extensible Stylesheet Language Transformations and is a language for transforming XML documents. Many Data Integration tools support XSLT and provide developers with additional features for XML data transformation. This is particularly useful if you use XML in your data integration layer, typically SOAP/XML web services, or if you use XML documents as sources or targets.

The main takeaway from this section about Data Transformation is that Data Integration Tools generally come with a large set of options and operations to manage Data Transformation. Solution Architects and Developers should ensure that:

- They determine the best pattern to transform the data as per business needs.
- Nevertheless, business logic that should be in target systems should not be put within the Data Integration Layer. Indeed, a Data Integration Layer should facilitate integration between applications, but should not be used to substitute for other applications.

Meta Data Management

The Data Integration layer, given the data it needs to operate, through data mapping and data transformation implementations, will load the data models, or have them defined by the developers. When doing so, the data integration layer is *de facto*, managing meta data. Meta Data is data providing information about the data itself, like the data model for example, the attribute list, or data model descriptions. Many Data Integration tools start to leverage this native feature to a more evolved one aimed at helping business users manage some data discovery or even data cataloging activity.

Chapter Four
Data Integration Patterns

Point to Point Integration

The most intuitive and primitive manner to integrate two applications is to directly link those applications. This is called one-to-one integration or point-to-point integration, sometimes abbreviated as P2P.

In this case, no dedicated data integration layer is needed because each application connects to the other through its own integration capabilities.

This "traditional" method of integrating applications offers a number of advantages, including:

- ✓ *Simplicity*: the easiest way to connect only two applications is to "draw" a direct link between them.
- ✓ *No additional tooling*: There is no need to add another layer (usually a Data Integration Tool) to manage this integration.
- ✓ *Pragmatic*: for a simple integration involving a very limited number of applications (typically 2) within a "closed" environment that is not meant to be extended or evolve over time.

Point-to-point integration has several advantages and can still be employed. However, the usage frame is quite limited, and organizations tend to have more complex and diverse information systems, with an increasing number of applications (generally much more than two), a growing technical complexity and protocols (multiple connectivity options depending on each application), and in a hybrid infrastructure environment (on-premises, cloud).

The more the number of applications to connect grows, the more the point-to-point integration pattern shows its limits and drawbacks, such as:

- The *n * (n-1)* issue:

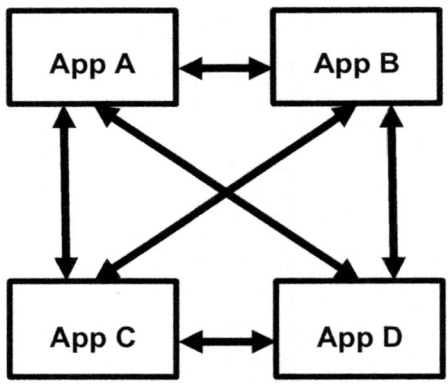

In this use case, we need to connect 4 applications: App A, B, C and D. If we count the number of possible integrations (arrows), we have 12 integrations to manage, which is 12 = 4*(4-1). We count two integrations for every bidirectional arrow.

This use case is purely theoretical, and in real life, you will not always connect all applications to all applications; however, it clearly and quickly shows the limits of point-to-point integration, which creates an increasing number of integrations and requires the development of a fully new integration for each business need.

- *Tight Coupling*: Point-to-point integration creates a de facto tight coupling situation between integrated applications. Indeed, if you operate a change in one application, an impact should be managed on the other.
- *Limited number of integrated applications*: point-to-point integration is incapable of handling orchestration use cases, especially if you have a business process that spans more than two applications.
- *"Spaghetti Bowl" effect*: The result of point-to-point integration in information systems is the famous "Spaghetti bowl" effect, leading to a "messy" integration situation, where it's extremely complex to maintain, monitor and respond in an agile manner to growing business needs in terms of data availability and integration.

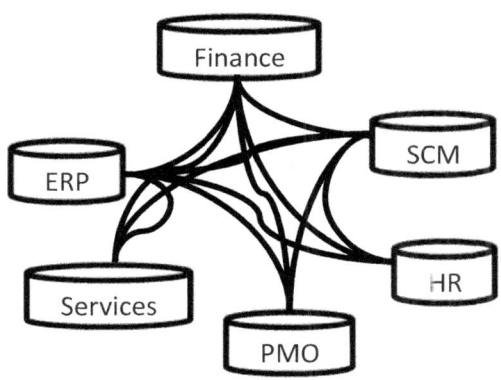

ETL: Extract, Transform, Load

Extract, Transform, Load is an orchestrated three-step process that extracts Data from one or more data sources, applies necessary transformations (cleaning, merging, sorting, filtering...) and loads the data into a target system.

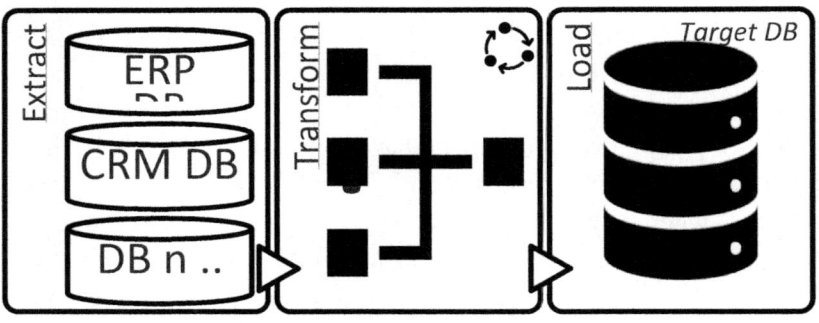

The ETL process in the above example will extract data from three sources: The ERP Database, the CRM database, and a third database. It will then utilize operation transformation procedures to generate a new data set that will be loaded in the target database.

EXTRACT

The extraction stage which comes first in the process, will extract data from one or more data sources. Each system might have its own data model, connectivity protocol and data format. Sources might include relational databases (the most typical case for ETL processes) or NoSQL databases. Data formats can include columnar data, XML, or JSON, and connectivity protocols can include, on top of databases connectors, web services or flat files.

This step (and all ETL processes in general) requires a certain attention to performance. Extracting a large amount of data might impact the performance of your data source as well as your process as a whole. A recommended practice is to ensure you do not affect source performance, as it might be a transactional database that is critical for business use, like an ERP database or a CRM database. In this regard, extract processes may guarantee the use of some optimizations:

-   *Full or Delta*: Full data loads are basically a copy of all the data, without applying filters.

    Let's assume Happy Tel needs an ETL process to run daily with the objective of analyzing customer data in a target tool (typically a Data Analytics tool).

    The first step of the process will be to extract data from the CRM database. A full load will consist in getting all of the customers' data from the CRM. If Happy Tel has 100.000.000+ subscribers, for example, this will imply a high load on the CRM database, perhaps impacting the performance of the tool currently in use by the customer service team.

    To optimize this, it's recommended to opt for a Delta load. If we have a closer look at the data extracted daily, we will find that 99%+ of it is **stable** (has not been impacted by any change in the last 24 hours): the vast majority of Happy Tel customers will not have their data changed every day.

The Delta load aims at identifying the **filtering** criteria that will allow the extraction process to get only the **subset** of data that has been updated in the last 24 hours, for example, by filtering on the data's last modification timestamp attribute. This attribute specifies the exact time when the last modification was made (this is only for illustration purposes; depending on your data, you may have other relevant filtering attributes).

This way, by introducing a filtering criterion to the extraction stage, your extract process will only extract the subset of the data that has been changed, optimizing the load on the database, the ETL process, and even the network.

One point should be taken into consideration: a full load might sometimes result in a high load on the source system due to the volume of the data. Delta loads, on the other hand, implying more complex queries, might lead to a high load on the source because of the computation capacity required to identify the delta set. As a result, you should make sure that your new query is not heavy to run on your system: In short, you need to find the right trade-off between a "light" query that will return a full data load and a potentially "heavy" query that will return a delta load.

- *Scheduling*: With increasing computing capacity (see Moore's Law), ETL processes can run more frequently like hourly or every 5 minutes.

- However, ETL processes are not meant for real-time data transfer as they involve a relatively heavy multi-step process and are generally triggered on a given datetime from the data integration layer. In this sense, they are neither "event driven" nor "on-demand" to ensure real-time action. More details on real-time integrations will be provided at a later stage.

The Extract step, which is the initial step of the ETL process, is launched at the scheduled time. To avoid high load on the applications and systems, it's recommended to determine the best "time window" for launching ETL processes. For that, the off-peak window should be privileged if possible. To identify the off-peak window, you need to have a good understanding of how your systems are loaded overtime. Typically, activity on applications is higher during the day when end-users and customers are active, but is lower at night or early in the morning, so you may take advantage of that decrease in application usage to run your scheduled tasks, for example, 1 am – 5 am. As always, there is no "one size fits all" time window: if your business operates 24/7, or across multiple time zones, you might need to choose a different suitable time window to accommodate those constraints. Another concern is that when running early morning or late night, you need to ensure proper monitoring is in place and that you have the required available capacity if you have business critical scheduled ETL processes that might fail or, worse, cause outages on source application during the Extract step.

TRANSFORM

After the Extract step, the second step in ETL processes is Transform. The Extract step will bring the data from the source, and the Transform step will perform the necessary transformations to make the data suitable for the target system and its data model. Data can undergo zero, one or multiple transformations:

- *Zero transformation*: In some cases, the ETL process can be a "passthrough", which means it extracts the data and loads it into the target system. A typical example is replication processes, where an exact copy from the source system is requested by the target system.
- *One-step transformation*: the data will be transformed in a single step by the process. You can look at the Data Transformation section for examples of how Data Transformation can be applied. In such cases, we generally apply a filtering rule for data cleansing or lookup operation to transcode data into target expected format.
- *Multi-step transformation*: this is the most common case, especially if you are loading the data from multiple data sources. It often entails:
  - o Bringing the data to a common target data model through jointures,
  - o Ensuring data cleansing through filtering and removing typically *null* values,
  - o Applying lookup when necessary to ensure data values are mapped to their corresponding counterparts as per target system usage,
  - o Applying aggregations in preparation of analytics processes,
  - o Applying deduplication through deterministic or probabilistic matching
  - o Or other types of transformation as described in the Data Transformation dedicated section.

Some cautions should be considered during the Transform step:

- *Encoding*: Data from different sources may have different encoding character sets: for example, the ERP Database will provide UTF-8 charsets, whereas the CRM Database will provide ISO-8859-1. You must ensure that your data is brought into a common charset that is also compatible with the target.
- *Edge or Corner Cases*: The ETL process may run with high volumes of data. This adds complexity when managing edge and corner cases, such as ensuring that the process runs correctly or through pertinent error in specific cases like empty data sets, or ensuring that classic errors (divide by zero, infinite loops..) do not happen. As you manage a large variety of data, such cases are more likely to occur, and data quality might be a concern.
- *Performance*: As seen in the previous step, performance is a critical consideration when building ETL processes. Performance optimizations should be considered by design, especially in multi-step processes, such as verifying that jointures are made on the right data keys or that the most discriminating exclusion criteria are applied to data as the first step to optimize the rest of the process.
- *Testing*: All of the above can be secured through thorough testing, ideally on representative data sets in terms of content and volume, so that encoding, edge cases and performance challenging situations are identified upfront and fixed in the development or testing phases.

LOAD

The Load step is the third and last phase of the ETL process. It consists in loading the transformed extracted data into the target system.

It is common that the target system is a Data Warehouse or a Data Lake, or more generally a data repository that will serve as a source of reporting and analytics use cases.

Data can also be kept in a **Staging database**, which is an intermediary temporary storage area for data before they are sent to their final destination. This architecture choice is beneficial for dealing with huge volumes of data from multiple sources that require multi-step transformations. In this case, a staging area allows more flexibility, consumes more disk space, but uses less memory and CPU than if all transformations were performed in memory. Another advantage for this design is that it allows data extraction from multiple sources at different times, so it can be reassembled in the staging area, go through needed transformations, and finally be loaded to the target. The staging database content is generally deleted after each process is completed.

Staging databases can also be a good option when you need to load data into multiple targets or also want to make your ETL process run in an independent way. Instead of having the three steps Extract, Transform, and Load run sequentially, the staging database can help you decorrelate the steps by loading the data into the staging area and transforming or loading them to the target at a different schedule than the extract one.

In the Load step, the following points should be considered:

- *Data Desync*: In case of data coming from multiple sources, extractions may not occur at the exact same time. In most cases, this might be fine; however, depending on your use case, you may need to pay special attention to this to avoid data set desynchronization if you want to apply jointures to data sets. Here is an example: You create a new customer A in your CRM at 9:05 and you bill your customer A from your ERP at 9:15. Assume your CRM extract step starts at 9:00 and your ERP extract step starts at 09:20. Assume that your target system is an Analytics tool, and your business users want to get a view on new customers and revenues. With the planned schedule, the data from CRM will not reflect Customer A, whereas your ERP data will reflect data on Customer A. Jointures between CRM and ERP data will not be applied on Customer A since this customer data is technically absent from CRM data because it was created only at 9:05 although the Extract step ran 5 minutes earlier, at 09:00. To avoid such cases, you can either ensure to run your ETL processes within an aligned schedule, or filter on a common "cut-off" date-time. In our previous example, even if data is extracted from ERP at 09:20, the applied filter would only request data from 09:00 backwards, so it's aligned with CRM datetime extraction.

- *Performance*: The Load step performance depends mainly on the target system, and in a symmetric manner to what was discussed in the Extract step, during the Load step, attention should be paid to the way you load the data: the volume of data loaded and the way they are loaded (particularly the queries launched on the target system) can impact the performance of your ETL process and your target system.

There are several optimization methods available to improve such operations:

- o *Incremental Loads*: Instead of doing a full data load, the ETL process can target incremental loads. Incremental loads guarantee that "just enough" data is sent to your target system rather than the entire data load. However, even in this case, certain full loads may still be required, particularly to initiate the target system data in the first place, and also regularly (every n runs) to palliate any data desync that might have happened and was not detected.

- o *Optimizing Insertion Operations*: when data are loaded into a target system, they are technically getting inserted into the system database. The insertion operation at the database level is costly because the database uses indexes. Indexes help make the search (and select) queries run faster, but they make insertion less optimal. If your ETL process performs a large number of insertions, it makes sense to optimize the insertion by temporarily deactivating the indexes or "dropping" and "rebuilding" them. It should be noted that this is more applicable to the target system where the Load operation is conducted directly at the database level.

ETL VARIANTS

The ETL process presented in the preceding section has some other variants that have been developed overtime.

ELT: Extract, load, transform:

In ELT (Extract, Load, Transform), the transformation is pushed at the end of the process, which means that it will run after the Load step in the target system directly.

This option can be a light and good one in case you have a target system that has scalable computing capacity. Cloud-managed databases and data warehouses, such as Google BigQuery or Amazon Redshift, can be a good fit for such a pattern. However, depending on the consumption, the usage cost can quickly rise, making this choice not cost-effective.

In general, ELT is not recommended as the main option since transforming data directly in the target system will generate extra load and impact its performance.

ELT is also not suitable if your architecture includes multiple target systems in which transformation steps need to be developed and maintained, possibly, each with its own connectivity layer, protocol and logic, posing maintainability challenges.

ET-LT: Extract Transform, Load Transform:

In ET-LT (Extract, Transform, Load, Transform), transformation occurs twice in the process, once after extraction and once after data load in the target system. The first three steps are the same as in ETL, however the fourth new step can help make "adjustments" to the data loaded in target.

Virtual ETL:

With the rise of Data Virtualization (a dedicated section on Data Virtualization is presented later in this book), the Virtual ETL pattern has come into play. In Virtual ETL, data is not copied from source to target; instead, the target system receives a virtual and logical view of the data in the source system.

This new pattern may be of interest during the exploration phase to avoid copying huge volumes of data, or when there are some legal constraints to copy the data as is; however, it does not replace classic ETL processes, which are primarily designed to physically copy the data from source(s) to target.

TEL: Transform, Extract, Load:

TEL stands for Transform, Extract, Load. In this ETL variant, the first step is to perform Data Transformation directly in the source system prior to proceeding with data extraction. Once the data is extracted, it is immediately sent to the target for loading without further transformation. This pattern might be suitable when you have a single data source and multiple targets with a source system supporting high processing power.

Reverse ETL:

ETL processes can address multiple use cases. Still the most common case is to Load data into Data warehouse from multiple data sources.

Reverse ETL reverses the process, extracting the data from the target (typically Datawarehouse) and sending it to the source. Such implementation can help with use cases of synchronization or data enrichment.

However, data propagation from Data warehouses is not always recommended, so Reverse ETL should be used with caution. Data warehouses generally do not contain the data as-is, but rather data following aggregation, calculation, curation, or other data transformations, causing data to lose its initial representation. Injecting that transformed data back into your production systems might imply data quality and data desync issues.

ETL USAGE

ETL is relatively an "old" pattern. It has been in use since the 70s and 80s and continues to be so today. It's considered robust, reliable, and suitable for feeding data analytics applications.

Production Source   Analytics Target

ETL allows for bulk data movement across multiple databases, with data warehouses and data lakes as targets in most common cases.

However, it is a heavy and intrusive process that can degrade the performance of source and/or target databases. ETL also introduces latency in the data integration process: making it ineffective for real-time or on-demand data access. It also implies tight coupling between target and sources as it is heavily dependent on databases: any change to the database schema might impact existing data flows, implying extensive retrofit.

SUMMARY OF CONSIDERATIONS WHEN USING ETL

Auditing: ETL are heavy processes that manipulate, transform, and move large loads of data. Logging and auditing can become very challenging because of this. Indeed, logging every step might take a lot of processing time and disk space, therefore the appropriate level of tracking should be determined in order to ensure the necessary details are captured but not too much to avoid excessive resource consumption.

Performance: As mentioned in previous sections (Extract, Transform, Load), performance is a key area of focus when designing and deploying ETL processes. ETL processes, generally handling massive data volumes, can cause performance issues on the Source systems during the Extract phase, on the Data Integration layer itself during the Transformation phase, on the target system during Load phase, and on the underlying infrastructure and network all along the process. Multiple optimization hints have been presented for each of the steps, and here are some additional practical hints:

- *Source and Target Database Optimizations*: ETL processes generally extract data from databases and load it into them (even though other types of data sources and targets are increasingly being employed, typically using web services, files or other types). Multiple levers can be used to optimize database performance, and they should be explored early on in the design phase to make an optimal design of your data integration. Operationally, DBAs (DataBase Administrators) can help identify indexes, partitions, triggers, and constraints that can be leveraged to optimize your queries, both in terms of extraction and to loading.

- *Data Volume Optimizations*: Data volume is a major driver of complexity and performance degradation. Optimizing data volume can help lighten the process end-to-end. Delta extractions and incremental loads can be a good alternative to full extractions and loads, reducing the impact on data bases, networks, and the data integration layer.

- *Bottleneck Analysis:* An ETL process involves multiple systems: the source(s), target(s), Data Integration layer and staging area, when applicable. In case of a performance issue, a bottleneck analysis should be conducted to determine which step of the process is taking most of the execution time and focus optimizations into that part of the process. You should note, however, that as you operate with complex and interdependent systems, a change in System A that will improve performance in the first step, for example, might have a negative impact on System B that will execute the last step. Thus, an end-to-end, holistic and global approach is also required, and a bottleneck can be dynamic and shift from one system to another depending on the design choices you make. Furthermore, based on many factors, you can have very different bottlenecks for two separate executions, which necessitate more robust and complete test plans to identify various cases.

- *Frequency*: The frequency of an ETL process is generally driven by business needs as well as technical feasibility. Traditional ETL processes run Daily or Weekly, and in some cases Hourly or Monthly. Increasing the batch frequency can sometimes improve performance, even if this might seem counter intuitive. The rationale works especially if the execution time does not increase linearly with the data volume. Let's take an example: if your ETL process takes 1 sec for 1000 records, it might take more than 10 seconds for 10000 records, depending on your algorithms: this indicates that the complexity of your processes (and their underlying algorithms) is not linear (may be quadratic or polynomial). In such a case, you may consider increasing the frequency of your runs and even going for micro-batches and higher frequency: for example, by making your process run every 5 minutes, you will finally have lighter executions and gain in terms of Data freshness.

Data Quality: Contrary to unitary operations, ETL processes handle large data sets. Data Quality might have various impacts on the ETL process: null or out-of-range values, as well as missing fields, can all affect your ETL processes while they're running. Hence, a good practice is to launch a data profiling activity, which will help you better understand your data set and identify any edge or corner case that you didn't think of. Thorough testing during integration and user acceptance are also effective practices that help overcome data quality issues.

Scalability: Scalability is the system's ability to dynamically adjust to growing volumes (or requests) by increasing its resources. While working on ETL processing and depending on your use case, you might face increasing volumes overtime. A possible solution to this might be ensuring scalability of your data integration layer. While this can help, it's very rarely that the Data Integration Layer constitutes the root cause of any performance degradation, and bottlenecks are generally related to sources and/or targets, therefore when considering scalability features, they should be evaluated on the overall design, not only locally on the data integration layer. In case of heavy and complex transformations executed by the Data Integration Layer, its scalability might help improve overall performance.

Batch Plan: If you are using multiple ETL data flows to move data between your applications, you need to build and document your batch plan.

ETL Proc. ID	Freq.	Start Hour	Target End Hour	Source	Target	Key Data Objects
P_01	Daily	06:00	06:15	ERP	Data warehouse	Customer Transactions
P_02	Daily	06:30	06:40	CRM	Data warehouse	Customer Master Data
P_03	Daily	06:45	07:00	Data warehouse	Data Visualization	Customer Transactions and Master Data
P_04	Daily	...	...	...	...	...

In the example above, a batch plan is presented with a list of ETL processes. P_01 will run daily at 06:00, extract customer transactions from the ERP and load them into the Data Warehouse with a target end hour of 06:15. 06:15 is an estimation, as the actual end hour may vary depending on the volumes, performance, network latency and other parameters. P_02 will start daily at 06:30 to extract customer master data from the CRM and load it into the Data Warehouse. P_02 should end by 06:40. Then, P_03 should operate at 06h45, extracting the data loaded in the Data Warehouse by P_01 and P_02 and loading it into the data visualization tool.

The batch P_03 should run after P_01 and P_02. What happens, though, if P_02 takes longer than expected and finishes after 06:45? Such a situation might occur if there is a delay in the extract or load steps, or if there is a particular increase in the data volume, making the end-to-end process longer. In this case, data transferred by P_03 (that runs at 06:45) might be incomplete or not in sync with the rest of the data. Having a consistent batch plan is essential, especially when there are interdependencies between ETL processes. Checks should be implemented to ensure that ETL processes that are dependent on previous ETL processes do not operate if their pre-requisites are not fulfilled, or if there are specific warnings, errors or notifications towards supervision, monitoring, or operations teams.

Transaction Management: As you load data sets into the target database, error handling should be a priority. Let's assume that you're going to load 1000 rows in a table within the target database. What happens if an error occurs on the 501st row?

- You have already loaded 500 rows. You stop the process once the error occurs, but keep the 500 rows loaded?
- You skip the 501st line and continue loading from the 502nd to 1000th line?
- You rollback the 500 rows that are already loaded and stop the process?

As you can see, there is no obvious answer, and no "one size fits all" solution; it all depends on your process and data. However, you need to ensure that you make the right design, especially if there are interdependencies between lines. Let's suppose we are trying to load the list of all customer transactions in Best Bank. If such an error occurs, it's better to go with option 3: manage a full rollback, making sure that the issue is solved, and relaunching the full process at a later time. Option 3 here makes sense because there are interdependencies between the lines, and the risk of data discrepancy is high if we do not have the entire data set. Let's take another example from Smart Electronics. Let's assume we want to load the entire list of 1000 new suppliers. If there is an issue with supplier 501, we can still load the rest and fix the issue for the supplier in row 501 afterwards. Hence, option 2 appears to be a suitable one as it will ensure we load 99,9% of the data, and as there are no interdependencies between the rows in this situation, such an approach is viable. In synthesis, during the design phase, the behavior regarding transaction management (how you manage the whole set of operations and how you handle errors) should be discussed and defined with the business in light of the constraints and possible options.

ETL USE CASES EXAMPLES

The classic: Feeding the Datawarehouse: The ETL pattern has been widely used to bring data from multiple business applications into the Datawarehouse. Business applications can be ERP – Enterprise Resource Planning, CRM – Customer Relationship Management tool, or any other application used by the business to support its operations (Billing, Financial Consolidation, HR Information System, Marketing tools...). A Data warehouse (DWH), on the other hand, is used for reporting purposes, providing a central component of business intelligence. A Data warehouse stores a copy of data from business applications, sometimes with a certain depth of history, and empowers business leaders in decision making processes through data analytics capabilities.

Let's look at an example from Smart Electronics, our manufacturer of electronic goods. Smart Electronics management requested their IT department to help them compute the on-time delivery KPI (Key Performance Indicator) for their suppliers. To do so, two main data sets are required: the suppliers' master data, committed delivery information and (effective) delivery tracking. These data sets might come from two or more different databases, such as the Suppliers Relationship Management tool (SRM) or Suppliers' Master Data database, as well as the ERP or any tool used to manage committed dates from suppliers (it can be in the SRM, or in the ERP, management as scheduling agreements), and finally to get the real delivery dates that can come from a dedicated tracking database or the ERP. Regardless of the names of the data sources, it's clear that in order to compute the requested KPI, data from multiple sources are requested.

To address this scenario, the designed ETL process will need to extract data from those sources and then load them into the Data warehouse, which will combine the data. The transformation step in the ETL process can typically aid in the lookup of suppliers' identifiers (as referenced in the tracking database) and the suppliers' names (as referenced in the suppliers' master data).

This ETL process's high-level design will look like this:

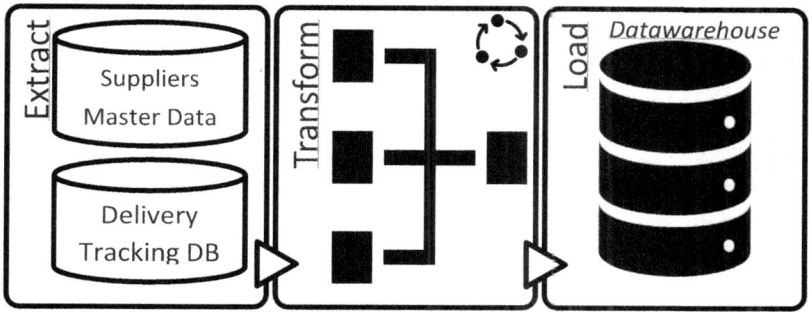

Here are some examples of data to be extracted from source systems during the Extract process.

- An example of Suppliers' Master Data (IDs and names are for illustration purposes only).

Supplier ID	Supplier Name
010203040	Smart Capacitors Inc.
010204051	Intelligent Circuits Ltd.
010203061	Integrated Sys Corp.
...	...

- An example of Delivery Tracking database dataset (Package reference are for illustration purposes. Dates are expressed in DD/MM/YYYY format.

Supplier ID	Package Reference	Committed Date	Delivery Date
010204051	001	03/04/2022	03/04/2022
010204051	003	05/05/2022	04/05/2022
010204051	005	07/09/2022	11/09/2022
010203040	011	21/07/2022	22/07/2022
010203040	018	23/10/2022	23/10/2022
010203061	101	17/11/2022	17/11/2022
...	...	...	...

During Transformation Step, two transformations are carried out:

- Dates are transformed from DD/MM/YYYY to MM/DD/YYYY format,
- A lookup to get Supplier Names from Supplier IDs is performed, using the data extracted from the Suppliers Master Data database.

At the completion of the Transformation process, we will have one result table. This result table will be loaded into the Data warehouse.

Supplier ID	Supplier	Pack. Ref.	Committed Date	Delivery Date
010204051	Intelligent Circuits Ltd.	001	04/03/2022	04/03/2022
010204051	Intelligent Circuits Ltd.	003	05/05/2022	05/04/2022
010204051	Intelligent Circuits Ltd.	005	09/07/2022	09/11/2022
010203040	Smart Capacitors Inc.	011	07/21/2022	07/22/2022
010203040	Smart Capacitors Inc.	018	10/23/2022	10/23/2022
010203061	Integrated Sys Corp.	101	11/17/2022	11/17/2022
...		...	...	...

During the load step, the previous result table will be loaded into the Data warehouse. This is the last step of the ETL process, which will be completed once the result table is loaded.

For the sake of clarity and to provide an end-to-end contextualized view, we will continue with this example until we explain how the Suppliers' on-time delivery KPI is computed. This computation, however, is not part of the ETL process. This also clarifies what should and should not be done within the Data Integration Layer, as well as the various design options.

Now that the result table is loaded in the Data warehouse, business rules will be applied to compute the needed KPIs.

The first business rule is to determine if a given package has been delivered on-time. For this, the following logic is implemented in the Data warehouse:

- If (delivery date ≤ committed date), then delivery is considered on-time.
- Else (meaning, if delivery data > committed date), then delivery is not considered on-time.

After applying this first business rule to our data set, we will obtain this updated result table (for better readability, the column Supplier ID is not shown).

Supplier	Pack. Ref.	Committed Date	Delivery Date	On-time delivery
Intelligent Circuits Ltd.	001	04/03/2022	04/03/2022	True
Intelligent Circuits Ltd.	003	05/05/2022	05/04/2022	True
Intelligent Circuits Ltd.	005	09/07/2022	09/11/2022	False
Smart Capacitors Inc.	011	07/21/2022	07/22/2022	False
Smart Capacitors Inc.	018	10/23/2022	10/23/2022	True
Integrated Sys Corp.	101	11/17/2022	11/17/2022	True
	...	...	...	

Packages 001, 018 and 101 were delivered on the exact committed date, they are on time. Package 003 was delivered earlier than the committed date, as per business rule, it's considered on time. Packages 005 and 011 are delivered after the committed date, and thus, they are not on time.

A new column is populated with the results of this business rule's execution, assigning True when delivery is declared on-time and False otherwise.

One might ask why this calculation is not done during the Transformation step in the ETL process, and why wait till this step to do it. This is an excellent question.

The easy answer to this question is "it's a design choice": we can do one way or the other. We had to pick an answer, so we went with the one in the example. But you are expecting a more detailed explanation, right?

Well, the explanation is that embedding business rules in the data integration layer is not a smart practice. If business rules are implemented within the business integration layer, it might seem at first as a quick win, but in the long run it will complicate the overall ETL process and generate complex maintainability issues.

One may argue that the design already included some transformation steps (date format change, lookup), so what makes this different? The answer is: In contrast to determining if a delivery is on time or not, Data format and lookup are pure data transformations that do not need interpretation of business logic.

Business rules evolve overtime as business needs evolve. A typical example here is that after a couple of months the business will find out that the computed KPI is not precise enough and will want to change some rule because:

- If delivery is one day late, it does not have a significant impact on the business, thus a tolerance of 1 day is included, and it is now considered on time if delivery date ≤ committed date + 1 day.
- Furthermore, the business has noted that when some suppliers saw their on-time delivery KPI impacted, they started delivery very early, which caused further issues in warehouse management, and the business started incurring costs related to stock management. Thus, if the delivery is received 5 days or more before the committed dates, it won't be considered on time.

As you can see, the business rule is much more complex. Technically, it can be added to the Data Integration layer during the ETL process' transformation step, but maintainability will be a real challenge in the long run. Also keep in mind that business rules can get increasingly complicated over time and typically, after some time, the business will find that a 5-day-early delivery is not considered on-time, but some exceptions might be made during certain periods of the year, such as the end-of-year period when logistics activities are stretched, and this will add another rule. Afterwards, the business might come up with another rule, claiming that these periods differ depending on geography. In short, those business rules will continue to evolve, and they should be managed within the Data warehouse itself, not the Data Integration Layer.

A second reason is that each information system component should be used for its intended purpose:

- Data Integration Layer: Data exchange and transformation feature,
- Data warehouse: storing enterprise-wide information and reporting (including KPI computation) purposes.

The second business rule to be implemented in the Data warehouse is that now that we have the on-time delivery information for each package, we can compute the KPI for each supplier, applying the following business logic: For each supplier,

$$On - time\ delivery\ KPI = \frac{number\ of\ packages\ considered\ on-time}{supplier's\ total\ number\ of\ packages}$$

On-time delivery KPI is expressed in percentage,

Which results in the following view:

Supplier	On-time delivery
Intelligent Circuits Ltd.	66,67%
Smart Capacitors Inc.	50,00%
Integrated Sys Corp.	100,00%
...	...

Intelligent Circuits Ltd. has 2 out of 3 deliveries on time, for a percentage of 66,67%. Smart Capacitors Inc has 1 out of 2 deliveries on time, for a percentage of 50%. Integrated Sys Corp. has 1 delivery out of 1 on-time, so 100%.

The business will use this provided data to make important business decisions. For example, the Sourcing department may decide to exclude any suppliers with less than a 60% on-time delivery rate. That's where you can see the tangible result of the whole process and also understand the importance of the data quality, the robustness of the ETL process and the soundness of business rules to drive efficient business decisions. Given the criticality of such decisions, the Sourcing department might want to iterate and update its business rules to ensure that they support the company operations in the right way. For example:

- Excluding any supplier having less than 10 deliveries per year from this calculation (as the KPI is not significant for low volumes).
- Providing a gradual answer to suppliers having a poor on-time delivery KPI
    o Sending a first level escalation when the on-time delivery KPI decreases to 80%
    o Sending a top management escalation when the on-time delivery KPI decreases to 70%
    o Cutting orders by 50% if the on-time delivery KPI decreases to 60%
    o Stopping all activity with the supplier if the on-time delivery KPI decreases to 50%

Reality is always more complex and nuanced because you might have a strategic supplier with whom you cannot stop all of your activities, but you might think about delay mitigation measures like applying penalties. Moreover, some suppliers might face exceptional circumstances that justify delays, in situations referred to as force majeure, such as unusual meteorological phenomenon that directly impacts their facilities like hurricanes or floods, and in this situation, you will not obviously apply the same decision-making process.

In summary, in this detailed example, the data integration layer is motorizing a critical business process by extracting data from multiple data sources, transforming it and loading it into the Data warehouse, applying an ETL, Extract Transform Load pattern. The data loaded is then interpreted to derive meaningful and useful information for business decision-making.

The ETL pattern can be used in other types of use cases. In the following paragraphs, two more use cases are discussed briefly. Even if the most obvious, classic, and widely observed usage is to feed Data warehouse, other usages can still be highlighted and for which the usage of ETL is "tactical":

   ✓   Data Migration use case: When a new tool is deployed in the information system, data migration can be required and the new tool must be fed with configuration and master data, as well as in some cases historical data. It can be also used when an application is replaced by another or when an application upgrade is needed. Other use cases might cover the M&A (Merger & Acquisition) context, in which a company merges with or acquires another company, requiring data convergence. For all those possible Data Migration use cases, the ETL pattern can be leveraged as "one-shot" usage during this migration phase. Contrary to classic use cases where the process runs in a recurrent manner (daily, weekly, monthly...), data migration is generally a non-recurrent activity and should be done only once. In such a situation, the Extract step will use pre-prepared data sets or a legacy tool, while the Load step will target the newly installed (or upgraded) application.

✓ Snapshots and historization: The ETL pattern can be used to manage snapshots and historization. This can be required for archiving or backup purposes. The Extract step will take place from one or multiple data sources, taking a "photo" or "snapshot" from the data. The Load step is meant to load data into an archive, a file system, or a database. Snapshots or history data can serve to provide a backup that can be leveraged if a damage or incident happens to the original database. Another usage is to store this data for later use, such as loading these snapshots into a Data Lake for hypothetical future Artificial Intelligence or Predictive Analytics use cases, where the depth of history in the provided data offers a powerful training dataset.

ESB, Enterprise Service Bus

The Enterprise Service Bus pattern is a Data Integration pattern that permits the integration of different, possibly heterogeneous, applications around a common communication channel: the data integration layer "the bus" or "the ESB".

The ESB pattern is often used to implement a Service-Oriented Architecture (SOA).

A Service-Oriented Architecture aims at implementing Services in the information system. A Service can be defined as a business-required functionality that can be accessed and executed remotely.

As stated in the SOA Manifesto, Service-Oriented Architectures implemented through ESB (Enterprise Service Bus) will tend to prioritize:

- ✓ **Business value** *vs* technical strategy: Business value should be the first driver when implementing ESB Data Integration approaches. The implementation should respond to real business needs, driving business outcomes rather than simply following some new technical trend.
- ✓ **Strategic goals** *vs* project-specific benefits: The ESB implementation in a SOA framework should look into "the big picture" and how it can drive strategic goals throughout the entire information system, rather than being simply a use case or project driven.
- ✓ **Intrinsic interoperability** *vs* custom integration: When adopting ESB as a data integration pattern applying SOA, the focus should be on increasing overall interoperability between the information system components, and custom integration should be avoided.

✓ **Shared services** *vs* specific-purpose implementations: the services established for ESB implementation should be shared and should favor reuse. In order to encourage reuse, services should be generic enough to serve more than a specific-purpose use case.

✓ **Flexibility** *vs* optimization: The SOA implementation through ESB should favor flexibility over optimization to ensure long-term maintainability and adaptability to new business needs and requests.

✓ **Evolutionary** refinement *vs* initial perfection: The SOA implementation through ESB is a journey, it is preferable to start small with strong foundations (Business value, flexibility, shared services, etc.) and evolve continuously, rather than aim for perfection from the start, which will impact flexibility and maintainability overtime.

For the sake of clarity with the terms used: SOA is an architectural style, while ESB is a data integration pattern that allows SOA architecture style to be applied. Multiple Data Integration tools support the ESB pattern and can assist in achieving this goal. The terms "ESB" and "Data Integration Layer applying ESB pattern" will be used interchangeably in the following paragraphs.

The ESB pattern will aim at providing services built on top of backends that can be called by front-ends to achieve business outcomes.

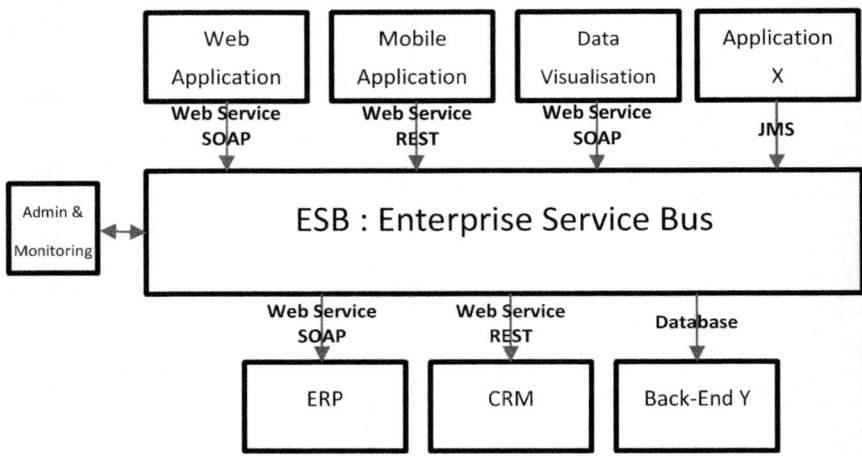

In the example above, we have an Enterprise Service Bus (Data Integration layer using the ESB pattern) connecting 7 applications.

Among these 7 applications, we have 4 Frontends, which will contact services on the ESB in order to fulfill their users' needs. Those frontends are "Web Application", "Mobile Application", "Data Visualization Tool" and an "Application X". These applications will often need to get data from the backend or remotely execute some services.

We also have 3 Backends among these 7 applications. These are the data providers and transactional systems that the Frontends might use to request data or launch some services. The 3 Backends are the "ERP" (Enterprise Resource Planning), the "CRM" (Customer Relationship Management) and "Backend Y".

Multiple use cases are conceivable with this architecture. Typically, we can imagine that the mobile application is a Frontend used by customers. In order to load the customer's profile in the Frontend, the mobile application will call, through the ESB, a service that we will name "getCustomerProfile". getCustomerProfile is an ESB-provided service exposed as a REST webservice that, when called in real-time, will call the backend via the ESB and the CRM REST Web service connector to retrieve the data and route it back to the mobile application, which will instantly get the customer profile and load it in the Frontend. This can be useful from a customer perspective as having a profile on the used mobile application will offer an enhanced customer experience through a personalized user journey.

Let's assume now that the customer who is using the mobile application needs to subscribe to a new service. Using the same logic, the mobile application will call a service on the ESB that we will name "subscribeNewService". As this information must be updated in the ERP and CRM, the ESB will then orchestrate two calls. The first call is to the ERP to initiate billing for the new service, and the second is to the CRM to update the customer profile. Once done, the ESB will instantly send an acknowledgment response to the mobile application, confirming the successful subscription of this new service.

In order to better visualize this example, here is a simplified sequence diagram.

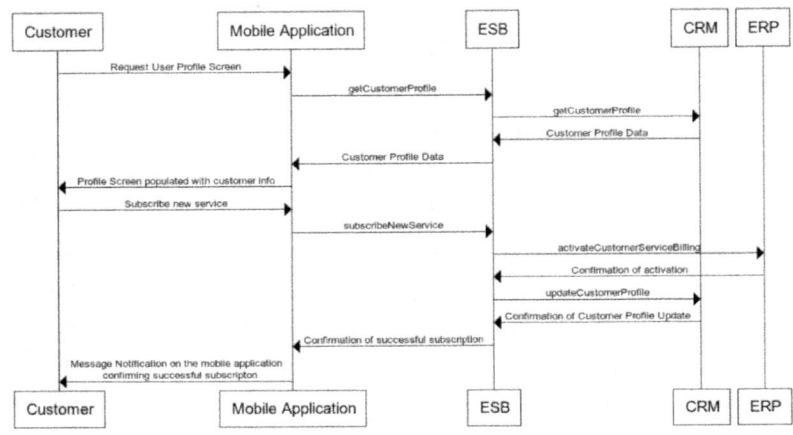

In this sequence diagram, multiple simplifications have been applied in order to keep it simple. For example, a customer must first go through authentication before they can use the mobile application; thus, in this example, we assume that authentication is already done. Furthermore, we consider that the call from the mobile application to the ESB is direct, however, it might be routed through a firewall, a security layer, an API gateway, or an API management layer. We also did not entirely adhere to the sequence diagram UML model, as some services need parameters (like Customer ID for getCustomerProfile or Customer ID and Service ID for subscribeNewService).

The first call to the ESB (Data Integration Layer applying the ESB pattern), is routed directly to the CRM. In this case, we can name this sub-pattern a "pass-through". A "pass-through" is simply a situation where the call from the Front-End is routed by the ESB to the Back-End with minimum, if any, transformation. This might seem as a low-value scenario, raising the question of why we use a Data Integration Layer in this situation while we can call the backend directly. The answer is that in order to favor reuse and service composition, as well as having a centralized platform to manage all integrations and mutualize supervision and monitoring efforts, it is still beneficial to go through the ESB.

The second part of the diagram consists in a call to the service subscribeNewService. The ESB will orchestrate two backends calls to execute this service. subscribeNewService is a service defined for business purposes, and it's not simply a technical service as presented in SOA principles. It is also reusable; normally, the Web Application can reuse it provided it has some customer portal capabilities, eliminating the development of specific services for each application and promoting reuse (shared services principle).

ESB USAGE

The Data Integration ESB pattern is suitable for:

✓ *Real-time or Near-real-time integrations*: contrary to ETL (Extract, Transform, Load), where runs are scheduled and can operate for relatively long durations (many seconds, minutes, or even hours in some cases), ESB integrations are generally real-time or near-real-time. "Real-time" means that the end-to-end call flow (from request to response) takes less than 0,4 seconds. Near-real-time integrations generally take 1 to 10 seconds. Real-time integrations are important for creating user-interactive applications, such as web or mobile applications that must interact with one or more backends while offering a smooth user experience.

✓ *Low Data Volumes*: In order to have the various services run at a reasonable time, the ESB pattern is suitable for low data volumes. Managing high volumes with ESB is technically possible, however it's not a recommended practice. There is no clear-cut definition of a "low data volume", but reasonably, each ESB call should be no more than 100 kilobytes. It can go up to a couple of megabytes, but if you find yourself reaching 10 megabytes or more per call, you should consider optimizing the data volume or think about another pattern like ETL that would be more appropriate.

✓ *High Frequency calls*: If you are looking for the right pattern to manage high frequency calls, for example more than 100 calls per second, the ESB pattern with Web services and API techniques can be your right pick. Indeed, the ESB pattern has been utilized in multiple industries, including Finance and Stock exchanges to manage high-frequency transactions, as well as telecommunications to manage users' services subscriptions or even charging.

Given the previous criteria, the ESB pattern is suitable for supporting data exchange between frontends and backends like Mobile Applications and Web Applications as frontends and legacy systems, databases, and transactional systems as backends. It provides, along with web services usage and definition of a service-oriented architecture, a reliable data integration layer, capable of supporting major use cases involving providing end users (customers, mobile application users, web application users) with a better user experience by allowing timely access to fresh data as well as an infinite set of service possibilities.

ESB USE CASE EXAMPLE

In this first example, you are a customer of Happy Tel, a mobile operator, and you are using its application to subscribe to a new music service.

When you subscribe to the new service, the mobile application will call the Data Integration layer (using ESB pattern) through web service to request subscription and provisioning of the service. Once done, you will receive confirmation that you have successfully subscribed to the new service and can start using it. The data integration layer serves as a middleware that will route requests and responses in real-time web service-based integration.

In this case, the data integration layer will offer a service that the mobile application will call, let's name it subscribeNewService. This same service might be reused by another frontend, often a self-service web portal where customers can subscribe to new services. Similarly, the CRM (Customer Relationship Management tool) can use the same service: suppose a customer calls customer service to request subscribing to the new music service; the operator taking the call can activate the new music service through the CRM, and the CRM will actually call the data integration layer, reusing the same service:

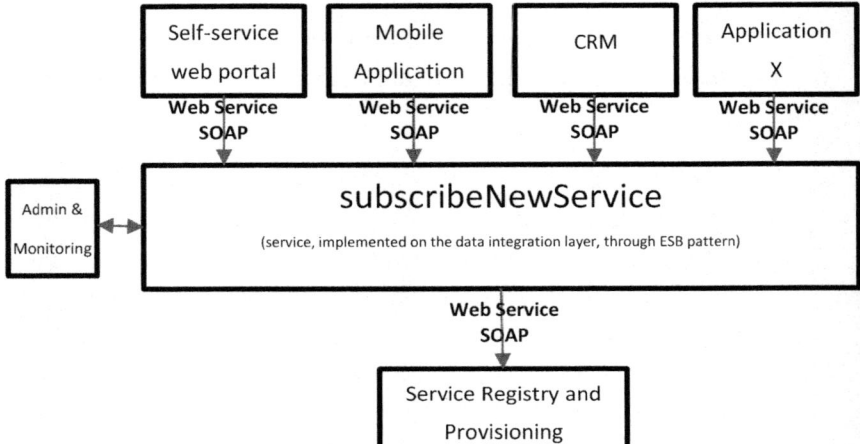

In the presented example, the same service can be used by four different frontends which imply a high reuse rate and show a great benefit of the ESB pattern usage.

In the second example, which is still based on Happy Tel, our mobile operator, a more global usage is presented to further demonstrate how the ESB pattern can be leveraged at a wider, enterprise level.

Happy Tel wants to transform its information system in order to become more competitive, offer a better user experience, and reduce its IT costs. It decides to implement a Data Integration Layer applying the ESB pattern. Here is a high-level architecture of the implementation.

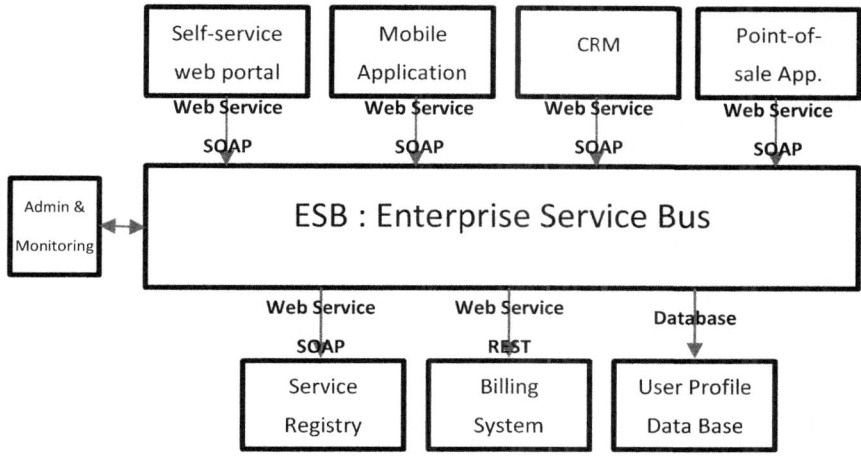

The applications presented are used for the following functional scopes:

- ✓ *Self-service web portal*: frontend, a web application that Happy Tel customers can access in order to subscribe to new services or obtain information like invoices and usage levels for services they have subscribed to.
- ✓ *Mobile application*: frontend, a mobile application that Happy Tel customers can install on their smartphones to get useful information about their contract usage as well as subscribe to new services.
- ✓ *CRM*: frontend, customer relationship management tool that is used by the customer service team as well as the sales team. CRM contains data about users, their contracts, and the services they have subscribed to, and allows the sales

team and customer service team to update customers' data and services.

- ✓ *Point-of-sale application*: frontend, application used by customer advisors in the shops and point of sales to subscribe new customers or respond to their requests when they visit Happy Tel shops.

- ✓ *Service Registry*: backend, a database that contains information about all users and the services to which they are currently subscribed. It's synchronized with the network to ensure every subscribed service is provisioned.

- ✓ *Billing system*: backend, tool used in order to generate customers' invoices based on their usage and subscribed services.

- ✓ User profile database: backend, a centralized database that contains customer information and profile data.

Happy Tel, as a mobile operator, has certainly more applications that are not represented here, such as an ERP, a Datawarehouse, a Data visualization or Business Intelligence tool, a GIS (Geographical Information System), a real-time charging tool for prepaid users, as well as various tools to interact with the network. In this example, we will stick to the applications presented in the illustration.

The following services have been implemented by Happy Tel at the data integration layer level to support multiple use cases,

Service	Description
getCustomerProfile	Provides the customer profile for a given customer, for example providing identity information and subscribed plans and services.
subscribeNewService	Allows a customer to subscribe to a new service, or a sales representative or a customer support team member to subscribe on the customer's behalf, for example, to a new music service.
changeTariffPlan	Allows a customer to change his Tariff Plan, for example changing from a one-hour monthly call plan to an unlimited plan.
terminateContract	Allows a customer to terminate his contract with Happy Tel.

Each of these services can be used by multiple frontends. This is a major benefit of the ESB pattern, which has a high reuse factor. A service is developed only once, but it can be reused for many use cases.

Service	Frontends
getCustomerProfile	Self-service portal, Mobile application, CRM, Point-of-sale App
subscribeNewService	Self-service portal, Mobile application, CRM, Point-of-sale App

changeTariffPlan	Self-service portal, Mobile application, CRM, Point-of-sale App
terminateContract	CRM, Point-of-sale App (a customer cannot terminate his contract in self-service mode).

Each service is then used by multiple frontends, but it can also call one or more backends.

Service	**Backends calls**
getCustomerProfile	User Profile Database: to get basic customer data Service Registry: to get customer active services ➔ The data integration layer orchestrates 2 calls, one to each backend in order to consolidate the full customer profile.
subscribeNewService	Service Registry: to store the new service activation and ensure its network provisioning Billing system: to ensure that the new service is billed to the customer ➔ The data integration layer orchestrates 2 calls, one to each backend in order to ensure that the full transaction is executed: the service has been subscribed

	to, and the service billing is activated.
changeTariffPlan	Billing system: to ensure the change of the tariff plan If the new tariff plan implies deactivating or activating new services, a call should also be done to update the services in the Service Registry. ➔ In this case, we have one call to the Billing system backend, and depending on the case (conditional transition), a second call to the service registry might be necessary.
terminateContract	Service Registry: to deactivate all the services Billing system: to terminate the contract and issue the final bill User Profile Database: to update customer profile with the contract termination information ➔ The data integration layer is orchestrating 3 calls in this case.

In this more generic example, we can see various types of services, the reuse factor, as well as the importance of the orchestration feature at the Data Integration layer pattern.

There are a few key points worth mentioning:

✓ *Transaction management*: transaction management is critical for the service "subscribeNewService". It means that, we cannot consider a transaction successful unless a certain number of sub-operations are fulfilled. Managing cases when the first call to the service registry is successful but the call to the billing system is not is problematic for our service. To handle this, we need to identify all cases as well as how to manage errors and rollbacks.

Status of first backend call to Service Registry	Status of second backend call to Billing System	Transaction Status	Rollback action
Failed	N/A	Failed	None
Successful	Failed	Failed	The data integration layer should rollback the first operation on the Service Registry. Otherwise, the customer will benefit from the service but will never be charged for it, generating a revenue loss for HappyTel
Successful	Successful	Successful	None.

It is critical in transaction management to manage all possible scenarios. There is another case in our example: what happens if the rollback action (second case) fails? This is a case that should also be defined, with actions such as ensuring that an alert or specific notification is thrown.

Furthermore, the more actions there are in a transaction, the more complex it is to manage its errors. Even though we will not go into detailed transaction management in this course, it's important to be aware of such a topic when building data flows on your data integration layer that have to manage transactions like payments or subscriptions management.

✓ *Exception & Error Handling*: some services presented by the data integration layer following the ESB pattern can be accessed via multiple frontends. These frontends are used by different users: CRM is used by the customer support team, whereas the mobile application is used directly by the customer. If the data integration layer's service fails, it will fail with an error. However, the same service is utilized by several frontends. In this case, each frontend should adapt the error message that it displays. Indeed, the error shown to the end customer on the mobile app can be "Contact Customer Service Support", yet the same error will make no sense if shown on the CRM to the Customer support team, who should have more detailed error information. Thus, when using an ESB pattern, and when a service is reused for multiple use cases, the error handling topic should be clearly defined, and error messages should be adapted at the frontend level.

EDI, Electronic Data Interchange

EDI, or Electronic Data Interchange has been introduced since the seventies. The main use case addressed by EDI is to automate data exchange between trading partners (Customers and Suppliers) for business documents, such as purchase orders and invoices as well as for payments and shipment information.

Here is a simple EDI use case in which Smart Electronics uses EDI to send Purchase Orders to Supplier S, and Supplier S sends corresponding invoices to Smart Electronics.

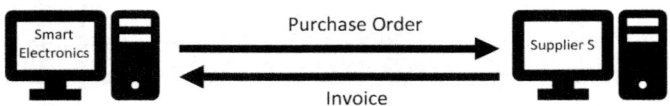

EDI follows specific message standards and formats like EDIFACT or X12 which are the main EDI message standards.

Other EDI standards have been developed for specific purposes or industries, such as:

- ✓ *ODETTE*: used in automotive industry in European countries
- ✓ *HL7*: used for healthcare data
- ✓ *IATA PATIS*: used to exchange passenger and airport data, and is maintained by the IATA (the International Air Transport Association)
- ✓ *SWIFT*: used for transaction and message exchanges in the financial and banking sectors.

X12

The X12 Electronic data interchange (EDI) standard is developed and maintained by the Accredited Standards Committee X12 (ASC X12), which is a standards organization. X12 enables interoperability between trading partners through standardized data exchange.

Initially focused on Supply chain and Finance data exchange like purchase orders or invoices, X12 covers today a large set of transactions for a variety of functional domains and industries.

Here are some examples of EDI X12 transactions in Finance and Supply Chain:

EDI Transaction	Data Object or purpose	Domain
810	Invoice	Finance
812	Credit/Debit Adjustment	Finance
820	Payment Order	Finance
850	Purchase Order	Supply chain
855	Purchase Order Acknowledgment	Supply chain
856	Ship Notice / Manifest	Supply chain
857	Shipment and Billing notice	Supply chain
862	Shipping schedule	Supply chain
945	Warehouse shipping Advice	Supply chain

Overall, there are 300+ EDI transaction sets, covering multiple needs. EDI X12 is widely used in North America, but less so elsewhere, where UN/EDIACT is the standard.

UN/EDIFACT

The United Nations/Electronic Data Interchange for Administration, Commerce and Transport (UN/EDIFACT) is an international standard for electronic data interchange (EDI) between information systems developed by the United Nations.

The UN/EDIFACT standard is used in many countries, particularly in Europe, but is less adopted in North America, where X12 is the standard. Its standard message structure allows it to be utilized across geographies and industries.

The following are some examples of document types used by the UN/EDIFACT standard:

Document type	Data object or purpose
DELFOR	Delivery Schedule
DESADV	Despatch Advice
INVOIC	Invoice
INVRPT	Inventory Report
ORDERS	Order
ORDCHG	Change Order
ORDRSP	Order Response
IFTSTA	Transport Status Message
INVRPT	Inventory Report
RECADV	Receiving Advice

Overall the UN/EDIFACT standard defines 200+ document type standards covering a wide range of business operations and transactions between business partners.

DATA TRANSMISSION & ARCHITECTURE OPTIONS

Nowadays, EDI is mainly transmitted via the internet. Multiple protocols can be used:

- ✓ FTP (File Transfer Protocol), as well as FTPS (FTP Secure) and SFTP (SSH FTP)
- ✓ Email
- ✓ HTTPS (and HTTP)
- ✓ AS2 (as well as AS1 and AS4)

As of today, AS2 (Applicability Statement 2) is the most adopted method. It ensures business-to-business data transmission over the internet in a secure and reliable manner.

Historically, AS2 was created in 2002 by the IETF (Internet Engineering Task Force), an open standards organization, and is specified in RFC 4130. AS2 has replaced AS1 that was defined in the 1990s.

Multiple protocols can coexist for a given trading partner connecting to multiple other trading partners.

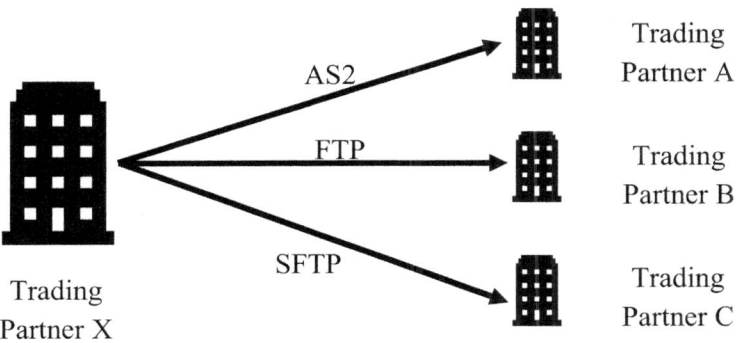

The transmission can be done directly between the trading partners, hence it is considered as "Direct EDI". Direct EDI is a peer-to-peer transmission, where a trading partner sends EDI messages directly to the other without any intermediary.

As presented in the schema above, Trading Partner X connects to three other trading partners, A, B and C, using direct EDI. Trading partner X uses AS2 to communicate with trading partner A, FTP to communicate with trading partner B and SFTP to communicate with trading partner C.

Direct EDI, however, has certain limitations as it may entail the maintainability of different links and integrations that are heterogeneous in case of a large number of trading partners since each trading partner might have a different transmission protocol or technology. Having a data integration layer with multiple EDI connectors and protocols can help you overcome this complexity (as shown in the schema below).

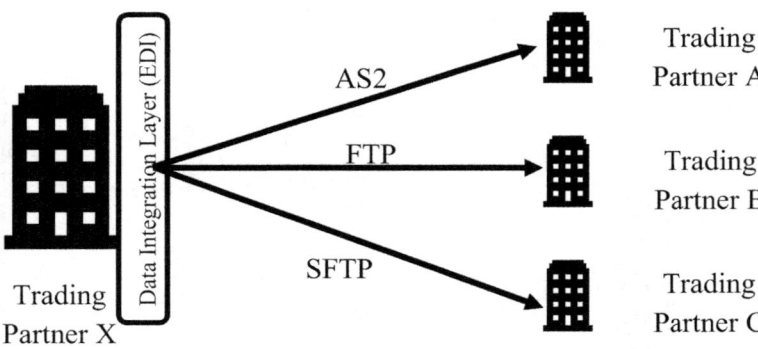

Another option would be to use Value Added Networks (or VANs). A VAN is a service offered by a third party that acts as an intermediary common layer between trading partners. In this case, a trading partner contracts the service with the VAN provider and routes its communications through the VAN, which in turn directs them to the target trading partner. The VAN, like a data integration layer within an information system, will "mask" the complexity of a direct integration. Using a VAN service, however, incurs a cost that must be paid by the Trading partner to the VAN service provider.

VANs are sometimes referred to as Trading Grids.

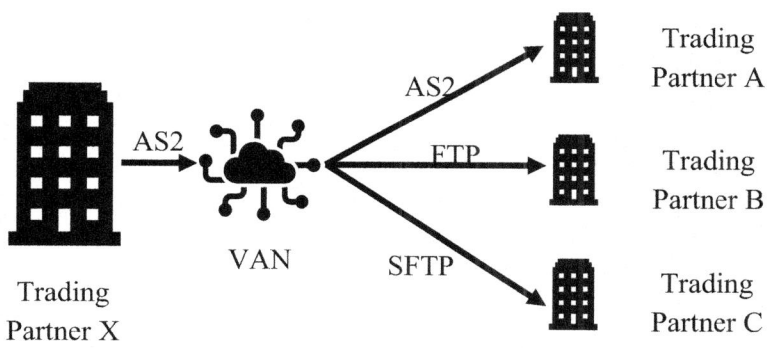

In this example, Trading partner X connects to the VAN by a single connector AS2, and the VAN connects to trading partners A, B and C via several protocols, providing a simplification layer from the perspective of trading partner X.

In practice, hybrid architecture is utilized by companies who use EDI massively with their customers and suppliers.

✓ A trading partner (let's call it X) will "impose" its message standard (X12, EDIFACT or other) on all of its suppliers. Its suppliers will have 2 options:

  o Use direct EDI by adjusting it to the trading partner's (X) requirements

  o Go through a VAN, whether recommended by the Trading partner (X) or not, to ensure that requirements of the Trading partner (X) are met

✓ The same trading partner (X), however, will have to adjust itself to his customers' requirements and connect to them via direct EDI or VAN.

The reasons for hybrid architectures include:

✓ *Supplier – Customer relationship*: in the market, a supplier generally lacks leverage with their customer, thus the customer "imposes" the way how EDI communication should take place.

✓ *Cost efficiency*: Depending on the number of transactions, using VAN can be costly. Let's say Smart Electronics will send an X12 850 message for each purchase order of a small and cheap electronic component like capacitors (say its unitary cost is less than 0,01US$), but as it will send plenty of orders, the VAN network will be heavily utilized. Let's assume the VAN provider will charge Smart Electronics 0,02US$ for each 100KC (Kilo Character). This might quickly become very costly, and there will be no positive business case for using VAN. As a result, Smart Electronics might decide to use Direct EDI to communicate with this supplier, avoiding paying extra fees to VANs that might significantly impact its costs. This is merely an example, and in this case, another option would be to optimize the purchasing process in order to integrate multiple components and quantities in a single purchase order and prevent having very small purchase orders.

✓ *Geographies of trading partners*: there is no "perfect" VAN. A VAN might be used in a given geography but not in others, in which case a trading partner might need to contract with numerous VANs or employ hybrid integrations to manage a worldwide supply chain.

✓ *Legacy and historical reasons*: EDI has been used since the 1970s and many changes have occurred since then. A given trading partner's technical choices and business needs may have evolved over the last five decades, implying technical debt, customized solutions and legacy usages, inducing a de facto hybrid situation.

EDI USAGE

Before implementing an EDI pattern in your Data Integration Layer, several usage considerations should be addressed.

First, you need to ensure that EDI is a good fit for your organization:

✓ *Is it used in your industry?* Some industries do not rely heavily on EDI, whereas others like the automotive industry do. Thus, before implementing an EDI pattern, make sure it is suitable for your industry.

✓ *Is it used by your customers?* If your customers solely use EDI, you might be obliged to implement an EDI pattern. Failure to do so may have an influence on your revenues and your relationship with your customer, causing your business to suffer in the long run.

✓ *Is it used by your suppliers?* This is not a major criterion to consider because since you are their customer, they will have to conform to your requirement. Even so, if you have a large number of suppliers, and many of them use EDI, there might be an opportunity to streamline your integrations through implementing it as well.

✓ *Are there any other alternatives if you do not want to use EDI?* In general, and more so, the answer is Yes. Alternatives mainly include Web services and API-based integrations, which are more modern and secure, but EDI still has advantages in terms of reliability and deliverability since it is persistent by design. It will also depend on your negotiation leverage with your trading partners.

If the previous assessment results in an EDI implementation, some key points should be considered:

✓ *Direct EDI or VAN*: depending on the use case, you can implement direct EDI, VAN, or a hybrid integration. If you have a large network of trading partners using the same VAN, subscribing to the same VAN provider can be a great option for accelerating your integration with your trading partners; however, if EDI is only imposed by a few of your customers, direct EDI can be a good option as well. Pros & cons should be assessed for each scenario before making a final decision.

✓ *Implementation Budget*: EDI implementation can be costly. When it is imposed by your trading partner, however, they bear the whole cost of the end-to-end impact. This can be an opportunity for a low-cost implementation. In all cases, trading partners should discuss cost sharing and agree on a clear "who pays for what" matrix.

✓ *My EDI, My Standard*: If you want to undertake a large-scale EDI project, you need to define your own standard. Of course, you can reuse existing standards like X12 or EDIFACT, but you will need to define the structure of the main messages, the mandatory fields for your business, the types of messages to be used (typically, purchase orders and invoices), and the default values to be used by your trading partners. All of this should be documented and kept on hand in case you need to on-board a new trading partner. This will make the process go much more smoothly for you. Furthermore, if your trading partner does not have a preferred integration, it can be adopted as such, making your integration easier. This, however, might not apply to your customers who can impose their own methods of operation, but if it works with your suppliers, it will already provide a certain rigor and standardization to your implementation.

✓ *Data Backups*: Unlike ETL and ESB, where data transits within the same information system and recoverability can be achieved by reviewing data in source systems, in EDI things can become more complex and especially, more impacting. Indeed, EDI generally delivers critical business documents, such as purchase orders, which a company cannot afford to lose, thus strong data backup and archiving methods should be implemented. Some service providers offer vault features, which are sometimes certified for certain regulations and have high security, integrity and confidentiality standards.

✓ *Business Case*: like any IT project (or just any project), you should assess your business case. EDI implementations are generally costly, both in terms of solution implementation perspective and coordination. Coordinating a project with multiple trading partners, each with one or more contact points, and each with its own interdependencies, constraints, and planning requirements, can quickly become a tricky project. Thus, before launching an EDI implementation, the project cost should be accurately assessed cand compared to benefits such as ensuring timely data transmission, avoiding human errors, or having a paperless process, to determine whether the business case is positive or not.

Data Virtualization

Data Virtualization is a new approach in Data Integration and Data Management globally. It allows retrieving data from one or more data sources without having to copy it, contrary to ETL pattern.

Data virtualization's main use case is to enable and accelerate data discovery and exploration. It allows data engineers, data analysts, data specialists and even business users to access the data and combine it without prior technical knowledge of the source systems, and without the creation of a replica of the data. The access is also real-time, providing you with an accurate view of the current state of the source systems.

Another use case that can be addressed by Data Virtualization is the implementation of logical Data warehouses. Unlike classic Data warehouses, logical ones do not copy data, but rather keep active pointers to the data that's needed in the source systems. At business users' request, the logical Data warehouse can deliver a (near-)real-time computed KPI or aggregation.

Data virtualization benefits include rapid and easy access to data and low-cost storage as there is no need to copy huge amounts of data, a democratized and governed data access.

On the other hand, data virtualization has some drawbacks too, such as affecting source system performance in case of heavy queries and not being suitable for managing large volumes of data.

Hybrid Patterns

When building a data flow, you generally chose one pattern or the other, depending on the business needs.

However, while building all your data flows, it might be impossible to stick to only one pattern.

From this perspective, you need a data integration layer that is in ability to support multiple patterns, and at least ESB and ETL patterns. EDI will also be mandatory in case you have integrations with your trading partners.

A different approach will be to implement a "specialized" data integration layer per pattern, meaning, implementing one data integration implementation for ESB, another for ETL, and another for EDI. This approach makes sense in case you have specific performance requirements or in case you want to split the usages.

CHAPTER FIVE
Connectors & Integration Mechanisms

Introduction

A Connector is a software layer that creates a link between applications to allow data transfer.

Connectors are a major topic in Data Integration as they determine a Data Integration Layer's capacity to connect to various applications, data sources, or back-ends.

There is a wide variety of connectors to handle a multitude of applications and protocols. This is an important criterion to consider when selecting a data integration layer, as it should provide connectors that will allow it to connect with your information system's applications efficiently and seamlessly.

Connectors can cover a large number of protocols and applications. Here are some examples:

- ✓ Relational Database connectors: connectors to RDBMS (Relational Database Management System), like Oracle, MySQL, PostgresSQL or Microsoft SQL Server…
- ✓ NoSQL Databases connectors: connectors to NoSQL databases such as MongoDB, Cassandra or MarkLogic.
- ✓ Business Solutions connectors: connectors that are dedicated to specific business solutions like SAP ERP.

- ✓ Technical connectors for specific protocols: including connectors to messaging layers (JMS) or Email (SMTP)
- ✓ SaaS connectors: connectors designed specifically for SaaS applications like Salesforce, Slack or ServiceNow
- ✓ Web Services: connectors for managing REST or SOAP Web services
- ✓ File management connectors
- ✓ Connectors to storage layer.

Connectors are sometimes referred to as Adapters. Some commercial Data Integration tools offer 700+ different connectors.

Database Connectors

Databases are organized sets of data that generally use a storage layer, from which data can be retrieved through "queries".

There are two main types of Databases:

- ✓ Relational databases: they use a predefined data model to organize data into tables of columns and rows. The data model is implemented upfront, prior to data loading. MySQL, Oracle, Postgres SQL or Microsoft SQL Server are examples of relational databases.
- ✓ NoSQL databases: they are non-relational databases that rely on a variety of paradigms to store the data, including Document stores, Key-value or Graph databases. NoSQL databases include databases like Couchbase, a key-value database, or MongoDB, a document store database, or Neo4j, a graph database.

DATABASE CONNECTORS FOR RELATIONAL DATABASES

For Relational Databases, Data Integration Database connectors will allow the execution of queries to:

- ✓ Get data from the Database using "SELECT" statements
- ✓ Add data to the Database using "INSERT" statements
- ✓ Update data in the Database using "UPDATE" statements
- ✓ Delete data from the database using "DELETE" statements

In a nutshell, a Database connector will allow you to interact with the Database in order to read and write the data you need, depending on your use case.

Database connectors might provide other queries like table creation or deletion, which have more specific/technical usages, and more globally, they directly execute SQL statements that might affect the database structure (ALTER, TRUNCATE ...).

Database connectors can also include features for calling stored procedures and functions, which is a good practice. Indeed, this promotes the usage of modular approach, avoiding direct dependency between the data integration layer and the database schema.

When connecting to the database, the connector provides configuration options that:

- ✓ Provide information to connect to the database, including the database URL and login credentials
- ✓ Timeout: the amount of time that the connector expects the database to respond to the query, or, if exceeded, to fail with a timeout error
- ✓ Other options include maximum connections, maximum rows to fetch for a given query, etc.

DATABASE CONNECTORS FOR NOSQL DATABASES

The operations offered by the connector might vary depending on the NoSQL Database to which the data integration layer is connected. For example, for a Document NoSQL database like MongoDB, the following operations might be available:

- ✓ Query Document
- ✓ Insert Document
- ✓ Update Document

In general, a database connector for a NoSQL database will allow you to interact with the database to read and write the data you require.

Contrary to relational databases, connectors in NoSQL databases may have certain limitations and/or lack of maturity.

CLOUD DATABASE CONNECTORS

Depending on the architecture of your information system, you might leverage cloud services providers to supply database solutions.

For Cloud databases, dedicated connectors may be required in some cases, depending on the cloud services provider and the chosen solution. In other cases, the cloud database provider might offer standard web services that can be used through standard web service connectors.

For databases like Amazon Redshift, Azure Cosmos DB or Snowflake for example, dedicated connectors are offered with some data integration tools.

ODBC AND JDBC

ODBC, or Open Database Connectivity, is a standard API (Application Programming Interface) for accessing databases.

Database connectors in data integration layers include an ODBC driver that acts as a translation layer between the data integration layer and the database.

For Data Integration Layers that use Java as underlying language, a "Java ODBC variant" exists: JDBC, Java Database Connectivity.

ODBC and JDBC are the underlying technical middleware that allows a database connector to connect the data integration layer to the database.

Web Service Connectors

A web service is a service offered by a target application to enable communication and data exchange at an application-level.

A web service connector provides the technical capability to remotely call web services of target applications.

There are mainly two types of webservices used when integrating applications through a data integration layer: REST and SOAP.

Other web services technologies exist, but they are not explicitly employed in the data integration context.

Web services are widely used in Data Integration, especially with the ESB pattern. They allow real-time (or near-real-time) integrations and are suitable for use over the internet and in hybrid architectures (Cloud, SaaS or on-premises).

From a Data Integration Layer perspective, a HTTP/HTTPS connector is the minimum requirement for calling remote web services. However, Data Integration tools offer more evolved connectors that directly implement REST or SOAP and provide a more suitable and quick way to integrate using web services.

In terms of architecture, web services enable the implementation of SOA (Service-oriented Architecture) and WOA (Web-oriented Architecture).

REST WEB SERVICES

REST, or Representational State Transfer, is a software architecture style for designing and communicating web applications.

A web service (or API) that follows REST principles is referred to as RESTful API. In the following sections, the terms REST web service and RESTful API will be used interchangeably.

A REST web service allows you to access a resource (data object, entity, etc.) via a URL (Uniform Resource Locator) [or web address].

REST web services employ a stateless protocol in a client-server architecture. Thus, sessions are not required.

REST web services can use multiple data formats, such as JSON or XML. JSON, however, is the most used format with REST web services.

REST web services can handle a variety of HTTP methods, including:

- ✓ GET: Get a representation of the target resource. The GET method is safe because it is a Read-only method and cannot cause the target resource to change. The GET method is also cacheable, which improves performance and scalability.
- ✓ PUT: Set the target resource as defined in the request (Create/Update).
- ✓ POST: Request the target resource to process the representation enclosed in the request.
- ✓ DELETE: Delete the target resource.

There are two major description languages that can provide a description of a given RESTful API's structure and expected parameters: WADL, Web Application Description Language and WSDL, Web Services Description Language. WADL and WSDL are both XML-based. Other description languages exist, but none of them are widely deployed or recognized as the main standard. Still, when supplied, WADL and WSDL can help accelerate the development on Data Integration tools by allowing the connector and operations definitions to be automatically populated.

SOAP WEB SERVICES

SOAP (Simple Object Access Protocol) is a messaging protocol for exchanging data in web service architectures over HTTP.

SOAP uses only XML formats in predefined schemas.

SOAP messages are XML (Extensible Markup Language) documents encapsulated into an envelope:

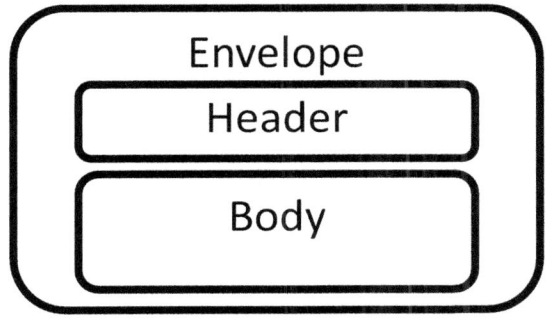

The envelope identifies the XML document as a SOAP message. It is used to encapsulate all the parts of the SOAP message.

The header contains header information. Header information is structured in blocks. The header is an optional part. Examples of information that can be provided by the header include authentication credentials, definition of complex types, and other parameters that might be used or referenced by the message itself.

The Body contains the "useful" exchanged data.

Optionally, response SOAP messages might contain a Fault element.

Here is a simple example of a SOAP message

```
<?xml version="1.0"?>
<SOAP-ENV:Envelope xmlns:SOAP-
ENV="http://www.w3.org/2001/12/soap-envelope" SOAP-
ENV:encodingStyle=" http://www.w3.org/2001/12/soap-
encoding">

<soap:Body>
        <bookWebservice xmlns="http://domainname.org/">
                <bookName>The Data Integration
Guide</bookName>
        </bookWebservice>
</soap:Body>
</SOAP-ENV:Envelope>
```

SOAP web services can be described and defined through WSDL (Web Services Description Language), an XML interface definition language.

The WSDL provides a complete description of the web service's operations, as well as full technical definitions of its input and output parameters and data structures. It is sometimes referred to as the web service signature.

In Data Integration tools, it is generally sufficient to load the WSDL within the development environment to have a pre-definition of all the operations that can be used, as well as their metadata (data schema and structure).

WSDL for SOAP is somehow equivalent to WADL for REST web services, even if technically WSDL can also be used with REST web services.

JSON FORMAT

JSON (JavaScript Object Notation) is a language-independent open standard file format that can be used with web services (especially REST web services).

JSON is defined based on RFC 8259 & ISO/IEC 21778:2017 standards.

The following data types are supported by JSON:

- ✓ *Number*: a signed decimal number (integer or floating-point)
- ✓ *String*: a sequence of zero or more Unicode characters. Strings are delimited with double-quotation marks.
- ✓ *Boolean*: either of the values true or false
- ✓ *Array*: an ordered list of zero or more values, each of which may be of any type. Arrays use square bracket notation with comma-separated elements.
- ✓ *Object*: a collection of name-value pairs (also known as key-value pairs), where the names (or keys) are strings. Objects are delimited by curly brackets, with commas separating each pair, and the colon ':' character separating the key or name from its value within each pair.

Here is an example of a JSON document from Smart Electronics that contains information about a purchase order, including products, quantities, and unit prices:

```
[{
  "product_name": "Capacitor 0.02F XZ",
  "supplier": "Acme 1 Inc",
  "quantity": 10,
  "unit_cost": "$0.2"
     }, {
  "product_name": "Capacitor 0.04F XY",
  "supplier": "Acme 1 Inc",
  "quantity": 15,
  "unit_cost": "$0.25"
     }, {
  "product_name": "motherboard Ref004R",
  "supplier": "Acme 1 Inc",
  "quantity": 1,
  "unit_cost": "$1.02"
}]
```

In this example, `product_name`, `supplier` and `unit_cost` are of data type string, whereas `quantity` is of data type number.

XML FORMAT

XML, or Extensible Markup Language is an open standard format for both REST web services and SOAP web services. It is the only format used for SOAP.

XML is defined based on W3C XML standards.

The following are the key concepts of the XML format:

✓ *Schema*: an XML file is validated against its XSD: XML Schema Document. The XSD provides a description of the accepted XML structure and content type.

✓ *Tag*: a markup construct that begins with < and ends with >. Examples:

  ○ Start tag, such as `<example>`

  ○ End tag, such as `</example>`

✓ *Attribute*: a markup construct consisting of a name-value pair within a tag.

  Example:

  `<customer id="117415">John Doe</customer>`

✓ *Element*: the main component of XML document: it's within a start and end tags and can contain child elements (and recursively more sub-elements). The content of the element is what is between its start and end tags.

Here is an example of an XML document giving subscriber information for a Happy Tel customer.

```
<?xml version='1.0' ?>
<subscriberInfo>
      <title>Ms. </title>
      <lastName>Smith</lastName>
      <firstName>Emma</firstName>
      <id>1002001</id>
      <balance>42</balance>
      <balanceCurrency>USD</balanceCurrency>
</subscriberInfo>
```

In this document, `<title>` is an example of a start tag, and `</balanceCurrency>` is an example of an end tag.

GRAPHQL CONNECTOR

GraphQL is a data query language developed by Facebook that has since been released as open source.

GraphQL provides a query language for the APIs and is considered as an alternative to REST. It is independent from the underlying storage or database and allows you to query data objects with the structure you request.

Here is an example of a simple request to get the name and balance of a customer having the id 1001 for Happy Tel.

```
{
  customer(id: "1001") {
    name
    balance
  }
}
```

And a related response, which follows the same structure,

```
{
  "data": {
    "customer": {
      "name": "John Smith",
      "balance": 42
    }
  }
}
```

In order to manage GraphQL queries, you need a dedicated GraphQL connector or a highly customizable web service connector.

ODATA CONNECTOR

OData, or Open Data Protocol is an open protocol for queryable RESTful Web services.

The version 4.0 has been standardized by OASIS, The Organization for the Advancement of Structured Information Standards

OData provides web services to query and retrieve data from compatible applications, relying on REST.

To consume OData, you can use a REST connector, but it is also possible to use an OData specific connector. Since it is specialized to OData, such a connector will accelerate your integration by simplifying configuration and offering better overall support.

Flat Files and File Management Connectors

Flat Files are a specific type of file that contains "human-readable" information, as opposed to binary files which are only "machine-readable".

Despite the widespread adoption of web services, flat files are still used in many data integration scenarios, particularly in legacy information systems.

The following are the most common flat file types utilized in Data Integration:

- ✓ CSV (comma-separated values) and delimited flat files: formatted like tables, with a separator between fields
- ✓ JSON: check previous section
- ✓ XML: check previous section
- ✓ TXT Files: Generic Flat File

A Flat File connector will allow you to perform certain actions on the file, including:

- ✓ Read a file and parse it
- ✓ Append more data to a file
- ✓ Create and write a new file

File Management connectors offer generic operations applicable to all files, whether flat or not. This generally covers:

- ✓ Create File: create a new file from scratch on a specified storage location
- ✓ Delete File: delete a given file,
- ✓ Rename File: change the name of a given file
- ✓ Copy File: copy a file in a given target location

- ✓ Touch File: change the file's last modification timestamp
- ✓ Check File Properties
- ✓ Compare files: generally using hash or checksums

It is also worth noting that data integration tools are increasingly supporting Excel files (XLS and XLSX). Even if they are not Flat Files, Data Integration tools are adding dedicated connectors to parse them.

Let's have a look at an example from Smart Electronics: Electronic components are supplied by Smart Components, a Smart Electronics provider. Smart Electronics will deliver purchase orders documents to Smart Components in the format of a flat file, CSV (Comma Separated), as shown below:

```
PRODUCTREF,PRODUCTNAME,UNITPRICEINUSD,QUANTITY
P00112,RESISTOR 20 OHM,0.03,100
P00034,CAPACITOR 0.1F,0.02,50
```

For better readability, the data in this CSV file is presented below in its equivalent, following tabular format:

PRODUCT REF	PRODUCTNAME	UNITPRICE INUSD	QUANTITY
P00112	RESISTOR 20 OHM	0.03	100
P00034	CAPACITOR 0.1F	0.02	50

However, usage of flat files is not a recommended practice, and web services should be the preferred data integration pattern when possible. However, it's still a pattern to consider in some cases like limitations of legacy systems that may not support the use of web services, for example, or that requires a certain level of data persistence.

Business Applications Connectors

In an enterprise information system, many solutions can be used to meet specific business needs, such as:

- ✓ ERP (Enterprise Resource Planning) that manages the company's operations and production cycles, as well as financials and accounting
- ✓ CRM (Customer Relationship Management)
- ✓ PLM (Product Lifecycle Management)
- ✓ Billing
- ✓ and many others

Some solutions might come with their own API (Application Programming Interface) and will necessitate the use of dedicated connectors. This could be owing to the way these applications communicate with other applications, or to the usage of specific file formats (Binary, semi-structured...).

Data Integration tools must connect with these applications as they are often cornerstones of the information system, and specific connectors may be required to fulfill this requirement. This applies to solutions like SAP ERP or Oracle Hyperion, where standard connectors will not work and a dedicated connector is needed.

Thus, when selecting a new data integration tool, it's critical to check the availability of suitable connectors for your business applications.

Some business applications will have standard interfaces, often via web services, and standard web service connectors will suffice to connect to those applications.

SaaS and Cloud-based Applications Connectors

SaaS, or software as a service, is a software model where the software is licensed to customers and end-users through a subscription and delivered by the service provider over the internet, as a service. All of the underlying technical layers (security, server instances...) are managed directly by the service provider, not by the customers or end-users.

SaaS has known significant growth and adoption in the past years. Nearly all information system requirements can be met with SaaS solutions: ERP, CRM, HRIS, Content Management or Data Platforms are just a few examples. As a result of this coverage and growth, companies that use SaaS solutions must integrate them with their information systems.

Because SaaS solutions are web-based and, in many cases, cloud-based, they generally offer web services to access their APIs. This allows them to benefit from the scalability and elasticity of cloud resources.

RESTful APIs are typically provided by SaaS solution vendors, and to a lesser extent, some will offer SOAP web services as well.

Standard web services connectors are sufficient to connect to SaaS web services. However, Data Integration tools vendors are increasingly offering dedicated connectors to major SaaS solutions. In this context, connectors have been built for SaaS solutions, such as Salesforce, a CRM SaaS provider, ServiceNow, an ITSM, IT Service Management SaaS provider, HubSpot, another CRM SaaS provider, and Expensya, a Spend Management SaaS provider.

Having such SaaS connectors dedicated to a given solution helps speed up the development process as it will simplify the integration compared to using a generic web service connector by automatically populating the operations list, metadata, and some configuration parameters.

Storage Connectors

The file management connector is designed to operate on the hard drive or storage mounted on the service, virtual machine, or instance on which the connector and the data integration layer are deployed.

With cloud adoption, new connectors are required to interact with storage solutions.

Depending on your environment, you may need to store files on Amazon Simple Storage Service (S3) or Microsoft Azure Blob Storage or Google Drive. These cloud services do not operate like classic hard drives, they require a dedicated connector with specific services to be able to operate with the data integration layer.

The operations and configuration options, such as authentication credentials, storage location identification, or data encoding depend on the solution.

It is recommended to limit the usage of these connectors to specific use cases and low-volume data storage. Indeed, Data Integration layers are meant to manage structured data rather than unstructured data and high-volume files. In case you need massive file transfer management, you can look for dedicated solutions like MFT (Managed File Transfer). If you use your data integration layer for massive-file transfers, you may encounter performance and latency issues, which may affect all transactions that go through it.

File Transfer Connectors

File transfer connectors can be leveraged for transferring files between servers.

FTP, or File Transfer Protocol, is the standard protocol to file transfer. Secured alternatives are SFTP and FTPS.

SFTP, or SSH File Transfer Protocol is an extension of SSH (Secure Shell Protocol) that allows for secure file transfer.

FTPS is an extension of FTP secured with TLS that uses encryption and SSL/TLS certificates.

The most common commands are:

- ✓ get: downloads a single file
- ✓ put: uploads a single file
- ✓ ren: renames or moves a file
- ✓ open: starts an FTP connection
- ✓ close: terminates an FTP connection

New protocols for file transfer have emerged with cloud solutions and as highlighted in previous sections, dedicated connectors are available to send files and interact with cloud-based storage solutions such as Amazon S3 or Microsoft Azure Blob Storage.

File transfer usage in the context of Data Integration should be limited and using a dedicated file transfer solution rather than incorporating all file transfer flows within the Data Integration layer may be a better alternative.

CDC Connectors

CDC, or Change Data Capture connector is a specific database connector that allows you to identify and capture the changes made on a given data set.

In order to detect and record changes, CDC connectors can employ a variety of techniques. For example, they can scan specific timestamps on the monitored tables or rely on the database log scanning.

Database log scanning is an interesting technique as it is non-intrusive. In contrast to other logics in which the CDC continuously scans the database data which might cause performance issues on the database, the log scanning technique has almost no impact on the database performance.

CDC is an interesting tool to support real-time change identification and can serve event-driven architectures, even with legacy applications.

Data Integration layers might not come with built-in CDC connectors. CDC connectors can be provided as additional plugins, add-ons, or as a third-party dedicated solution such as Debezium open-source solution, and their use can be more complicated than usual connectors as they may entail installing agent-like software at the database level.

Email Connectors

Emails can be required in Data Integration use cases to send notifications to end users when raising alerts or simply to provide information to a specific group.

In order to interact with emails, Data Integration layers rely on dedicated connectors. These connectors will support POP or IMAP protocols to get and read incoming emails, as well as SMTP to send emails.

POP or IMAP connectors will allow you to configure access credentials to be able to read the emails.

The SMTP connector will provide you with several options when sending an email:

- ✓ Format: Plain Text or HTML
- ✓ To, From, CC and BCC parameters
- ✓ SMTP server configuration (credentials, URL, Port, SSL/TLS ...)
- ✓ Attachment management

Some Data Integration layers might offer connectors specific to some email service providers like Gmail connector.

Additionally, with SaaS solutions providing emailing services, such as Mailjet, Sendinblue or MailChimp, SaaS vendors start to offer web services that the data integration layer can use to send emails or retrieve data about email campaigns. In this case, a web service connector should be used instead of classic email connectors. In a few cases, your Data Integration tool may have a specific connector for a particular SaaS solution, making integration even easier.

Messaging Connectors

MOM, or Message-oriented Middleware, enables message exchanges between applications supporting messaging protocols.

MOM can be considered as a Data Integration Layer; however, its capability is limited to message exchanges.

Communication in the MOM model follows the Publish/Subscribe paradigm. They are sometimes referred to as Pub/Sub middleware. The message is published (or produced) by the publisher application (or module) and consumed by the subscriber application (or module).

MOM has two main patterns:

✓ Queues: a point-to-point pattern in which a message is published on a specific queue by the published application to which a consuming subscribed application connects to receive the message.

✓ Topics: one-to-many or broadcast models, in which a published message can be consumed by several applications.

There are pros and cons to using queues or topics; queues ensure better deliverability, whereas topics are better suited for broadcasting.

A MOM relies on a storage area to keep queues and topics, as well as messages, until they are consumed. In this regard, they differ from standard data integration layers, which often do not rely heavily on storage and instead focus only on synchronous data exchange. MOM supports asynchronous integrations, which are useful in fault-tolerant architectures: indeed, a message that is published on a queue or topic, will "wait" till it's consumed. If the consuming application is down or unavailable for some reason, message delivery is delayed and asynchronous as it will not occur until the application is up again.

Depending on architecture choices, MOM can operate in full autonomy or as an add-on to Data Integration Layers to augment their technical capability.

In order for a Data Integration Layer to connect with a MOM, a messaging connector is required. This connector can communicate in two ways: publish messages or subscribe and receive messages.

Multiple messaging standards have been published. The most important and adopted one is JMS, or Java Messaging Service (or Jakarta messaging). Some proprietary solutions use JMS as an underlying component, on top of which additional features are built. Another important standard is MQTT (Message Queuing Telemetry Transport), a network protocol that runs over TCP/IP and is standardized by OASIS.

Examples of MOM solutions include Azure Service Bus, Tibco EMS, Solace, Apache Kafka, and many others.

From the Data Integration Layer perspective, the messaging connector will offer features such as:

- ✓ Create a queue
- ✓ Publish a message on a queue
- ✓ Receive a message from a queue
- ✓ Publish a message on a topic
- ✓ Subscribe to a topic

MOM is an important enabler in an information system that can offer multiple perspectives. Typically, MOM enables event-driven architectures. Coupling a CDC (Change Data Capture) component with a MOM can give powerful features to timely detect changes and events in a given application and propagate them to other applications in real-time.

Functionally, with CDC employing non-intrusive log scanners and MOM using listeners to receive messages timely, numerous use cases like building a real-time dashboard or propagating in real-time master data changes to multiple applications become possible.

However, MOM used in a standalone model without being combined with a more global and functionally rich Data Integration layer may suffer from limited integration capabilities because natively, MOM are not designed to handle many connectors and hybrid integrations and are better suitable to only manage messaging. Such usage can be interesting between applications who natively support MOM integrations, via JMS for example.

Connector SDK

Even though your Data Integration Layer provides hundreds of connectors, there might be applications in your information system that won't be compatible with any of them. This can be due to a variety of reasons, including the use of a deprecated software version, a very old legacy system, or a modern tool with very specific API and integration features.

In this case, the following options should be considered:

✓ Not connecting to your application: this can be an option if the business need is not considered important, or if the application is planned for decommissioning for example.

✓ Connecting with degraded mode: for example, using files or non-secure protocols. This is not recommended, but depending on your constraints and requirements, it can be a pragmatic trade-off.

✓ Requesting that the application complies with a standard integration model, such as requesting the application team to implement web services to permit integration; this, however, will incur a cost, and might not be possible if you do not have access to the application code due to legal or compliance reasons (proprietary software for example, or SaaS based software that do not offer customization features).

✓ Requesting your Data Integration Tool software vendor to include this connector in one of his next releases: this might depend on your software vendor's roadmap as well as your negotiation leverage. In case of an Open-source solution, you can ask for support from the community. It is also possible that your data integration tool software vendor can provide you with access to a non-supported connector that might be still under development, in beta release, or simply deprecated and no longer supported, but that you can use at your own discretion and risk. In such cases you need to ensure proper security testing to avoid any possible vulnerability.

There is, however, another option: what if you develop the connector to your application yourself? If your data integration layer offers a connector SDK (Software Development Kit), this could be a viable alternative.

A connector SDK (Software Development Kit) is a toolkit provided by the data integration tool vendor to help build customized connectors. The development activities should happen in the data integration tool's language. In many cases, Java is supported, and to speed up the connector's development, you can generally use existing libraries that provide out-of-the-box connector features.

However, not all data integration tools offer a connector SDK, so keep that feature in mind when assessing tool choice.

Other Connectors

You can use a large number of connectors to connect your applications to your data integration layer. So far, we discussed Relational database connectors, NoSQL database connectors, SOAP Web services connectors, REST web services connectors, GraphQL connectors, OData connectors, File management connectors, flat files connectors, business applications connectors, SaaS and cloud-based application connectors, storage connectors, FTP, SFTP and FTPS connectors, CDC connectors, SMTP and Email connectors as well as messaging connectors. But, even with all these connectors, some applications may remain inaccessible, necessitating the creation of a dedicated connector using the connector SDK.

This shows how diverse integrations can be, and the more applications you have, the more connectors you might require, especially if you have a hybrid information system with legacy and modern applications, some on-premises, some hosted in your private cloud, some in the public cloud, or some that are SaaS based.

To address this diversity, new connectors continue to be released and added to the data integration tools to ensure better coverage of the various applications. Some of them are discussed in the following sections.

AS2 CONNECTOR

AS2, or Applicability Statement 2, is used in the EDI context. This has been presented and discussed in the EDI section. The AS2 connector is a connector that can be used in this context of EDI B2B data exchanges.

DIAMETER CONNECTOR

Diameter is an application layer network protocol that is mostly utilized in the telecommunication industry. It supports integration between business applications and operations and network systems. It is used for many of the interfaces defined in the 3GPP standard (3rd Generation Partnership Project), which is known for the development of 2G, 2.5G, 3G, 4G and 5G telecommunication standards.

A diameter connector is one that allows communication with diameter protocols.

LDAP CONNECTOR

LDAP, or Lightweight directory access protocol, is an application protocol that allows users to access and maintain directory services. A directory is typically used to store organization information in a central repository, namely user and identity information like usernames, passwords, emails, locations, and phone numbers.

An LDAP connector allows a data integration layer to connect to a target directory, search and retrieve information, and in some situations, directly manage the directory by adding, updating, or deleting information.

GROOVY CONNECTOR

Apache Groovy is a concise language for Java that adds a certain level of simplicity in building custom scripts. A groovy connector provides Groovy code execution capability to the data integration layer.

CHAPTER SIX
Security & Technical Architecture

Security

Security should be a top priority when designing and implementing a data integration layer and each of the Data Flows in this data integration layer.

As data flows from application A to application B, it's critical to consider security aspects from an end-to-end perspective. Is the access to the data secure? Is the authentication method robust? Is an encryption algorithm applied to the transferred data? Is the data secure and its integrity preserved while being transported?

According to the Ponemon Institute, the average cost of a data breach in 2022 is $4.24 million. A data breach cost can be a sum of many factors, including brand impact, penalties to customers or trading partners, legal costs, etc.

In short, anticipation is important to avoid any data breach, and your data flows and data integration layer should be secured as much as possible to limit any data breach risk that could damage your organization.

To ensure secure data flows in your integration, security topics should be considered from and end-to-end perspective during design and architecture phases. This does not guarantee the security of all data in your information system because that is also dependent on the security of each application and its data, but it is a cornerstone to having secure data exchanges, which, for cyber attackers and hackers, is considered a "convenient" opportunity to sniff your data through man-in-the-middle attack schemes.

The design should follow the privacy-by-design and security-by-design principles. It's also recommended to rely on published and recognized standards and frameworks such as OWASP (Open Web Application Security Project), to secure those requirements.

AUTHENTICATION

Authentication mechanisms are used to prove the identity of the requester, whether it is an application or a user, for a given application on which a request is made.

In the following use case, authentication should be considered at two points:

- ✓ When the frontend calls the data integration layer
- ✓ When the data integration layer calls the backend

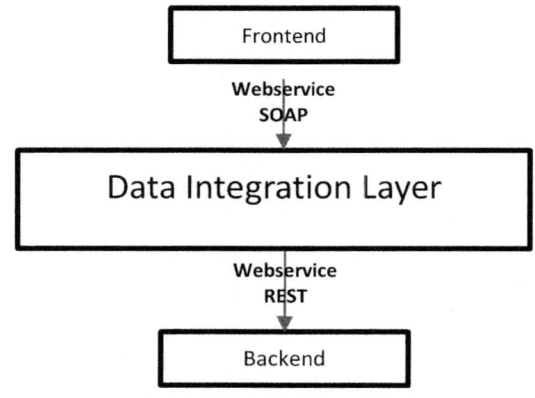

The data integration layer generally supports only one authentication mechanism for frontends (meaning, when the data integration layer is exposing the (web) service) for two reasons:

✓ *Standardization*: a data integration layer is introduced in an information system architecture to "put order" and "reduce entropy". From this perspective, there is generally an agreed-upon set of security patterns and standards to unify the way applications connect to the data integration layer.

✓ *Technical Constraint*: Data integration layers with the technical capability to expose web services will rely on a web application server with an authentication configuration that is instantiated once launched and cannot be dynamically changed (on-the-fly). In case you must provide more than one authentication option, this technical constraint can be lifted by implementing dedicated web application server per authentication mechanism, even though it is not recommended.

This only applies to the frontend connecting to the data integration layer, but not to the data integration layer calling the backend.

Moreover, the above is not applicable in cases where the used pattern is ETL because the data integration layer in ETL does not provide web services, unlike in the case of the ESB pattern.

When calling the backend, there are many types of authentication, depending on the application you are connecting to:

✓ For web services and integrations over HTTP, authentication can be based on credentials (user/passwords), secret keys (API keys), authentication tokens or certificates.

✓ For databases, user/password credentials are usually used to manage authentication.

✓ For business applications you might have specific mechanisms, but still relying generally on credentials (user/passwords) or certificates.

When designing a data flow, authentication information should be gathered at an early stage to ensure it is supported by the data integration layer and that it is a secure authentication method.

Note that having an authentication method does not always guarantee that the data flow is fully secure: some authentication mechanisms are weak or obsolete, such as HTTP Basic Authentication, where the credentials are not encrypted, and confidentiality of data is not ensured. Thus, when selecting an authentication method, security constraints, data integration layer capabilities (and constraints), and business impacts should all be considered. In case you are using SSL/TLS certificates you should also ensure you have a policy of revoking and renewing certificates.

ENCRYPTION

Encryption is used in data integration in order to encode the initial data load into a different representation that can only be decoded by the legitimate target recipient application.

While data is being transferred in a data integration context, encryption is applied, during the transfer. This does not, however, imply that the data is "encrypted at rest". Encryption at rest refers to the encryption of data while it is persisted and stored in a source or target application (or database). This feature is not provided by the data integration layer, but by the applications themselves. The data integration layer can only manage the data encryption during the exchange process.

For web service-based integrations, using HTTPS is recommended (instead of HTTP). HTTPS or HyperText Transfer Protocol Secure, is the extension of HTTP with the usage of TLS (Transport Layer Security) to encrypt data and ensure confidentiality, integrity, and authenticity through the use of certificates.

SECURITY CHECKLIST

When it comes to security in data integration, there are several options, depending on security risk assessments, available technical solutions, organizations' policies, industry standards and business needs and impacts.

In order to maintain consistency across the organization, it is critical to establish the security "checklist" with your security (and compliance) department and skills specialists and experts. Your checklist should describe the security requirements, patterns, main technical choices and the standards that will be applied.

For example, if you integrate patients' health insurance data, the pattern must ensure end-to-end data encryption, strong authentication protocol and more globally align with HIPAA (Health Insurance Portability and Accountability Act) guidelines, whereas if you are simply collecting open data from a publicly accessible data repository, you can use less complex mechanisms.

The defined checklist and patterns should be applied systematically. In case of exceptions, ensure a proper derogation policy is in place and ensure that the risk is properly assessed before confirming the exception.

Compliance requirements should be considered as well. Based on the data type and sensitivity, the industry in which you operate, and your commitments towards you customers, you might apply additional or specific measures, especially when it comes to personal data, bank and finance data or health data.

The security checklist should continue to be updated regularly. Security protocols are subject to recurrent updates, and in some cases, breaches. The Heartbleed bug is a good example in this regard: the Heartbleed bug is a serious vulnerability in OpenSSL, which was used to secure communications encrypted by SSL/TLS.

Standards and frameworks, like ISO 27001 can help you put the right controls and policies for an optimal information security management, as well as regular security audits, penetration testing and vulnerability testing to ensure the application of a continuous improvement loop.

Technical Architecture

Technical Architecture defines the underlying infrastructure on which your Data Integration will run.

It generally responds to non-functional requirements for your Data Integration Layer, such as Availability, Performance, Security and Network.

AVAILABILITY

Availability is the probability of a particular system providing the expected service at a satisfactory level of operational performance. Highly accessible systems generally have an availability higher than 99,99% (sometimes referred to as "four nines"). Such availability necessitates changes to the technical architecture in order to remove SPOF (Single Points Of Failure) and implement redundancy mechanisms to ensure resiliency and reliable emergency backup in case of failure.

The following table illustrates the corresponding "acceptable" downtime for a given availability:

Availability	Downtime per year	Downtime per day
99% (two nines)	3.65 days	14.4 minutes
99.9% (three nines)	8.77 hours	1.44 minutes
99.99% (four nines)	52.6 minutes	8.64 seconds
99.999% (five nines)	5.26 minutes	864 milliseconds

TECHNICAL ARCHITECTURE FOR HIGH AVAILABILITY

Let's start with an example of a problem statement. Assume you need to implement a Data Integration Layer with a 99,99% availability (this means it can have a downtime of 1 second every 1000 seconds, or 8.64 seconds every day).

Let's also assume that only servers (or virtual machines, or cloud instances) with 99% uptime (or availability) are accessible. How can we achieve high availability of 99,99%?

Let p be the probability of failure (or downtime) for one available server: $p = \frac{1}{100}$.

If we use two servers in "parallel" instead of one, the probability of failure of the system, let's name it p_s is:

$$p_s = \frac{1}{100} \times \frac{1}{100} = \frac{1}{10000} = 0,0001.$$

This gives us an availability of:

$$a_s = 1 - p_s = 1 - 0,0001 = 0,9999 = 99,99\%$$

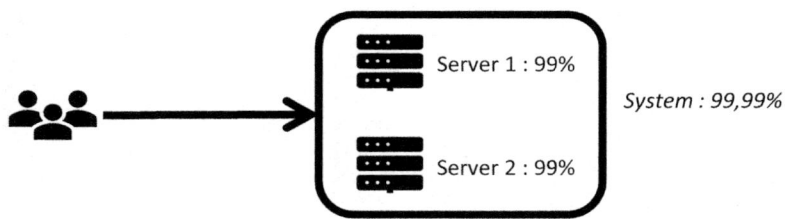

LOAD BALANCING AND CLUSTERING

To implement such architectures, we need a more sophisticated setup and configurations, as running two servers "in parallel" is not simple. There are two basic non-exclusive architecture options to consider:

✓ *Load Balancing*: a load balancer is an equipment (or software) that allows requests to be distributed across two or more servers (or nodes) following a specific algorithm like round-robin. This can be achieved through a physical load balancer such as BigIP F5 or a software load balancer such as HAProxy. The availability of the load balancer itself should be considered when calculating the availability of the overall system (System = Servers + Load balancer). The Load Balancer can constitute in some cases the Single Point of Failure of your system.

✓ *Clustering*: a cluster is a technical grouping of numerous servers (or nodes), viewed as a single system and deployed to improve availability and performance.

ACTIVE/ACTIVE VS ACTIVE/PASSIVE

Several approaches exist to ensure high availability, with the two main paradigms being:

✓ *Active/Active* : two or more nodes (or servers) are "up" at the same time, and as requests arrive, they are distributed between the nodes, generally processing behind a load balancer that routes the requests based on predefined algorithms such as round-robin. In case one node fails, the remaining nodes will continue to operate and process requests, and the algorithm will adjust the distribution of requests to optimize the usage of available resources.

✓ *Active/Passive*: the nodes are part of the same cluster. At a given time, one node is up (active node), and the rest are in "stand by" mode (or "warm" state). If the active node crashes, "goes down", or simply can't handle the request, a "stand by" node goes up and responds to the request (and next ones) till the initial node recovers. Starting the "warm" node however might imply additional time during which no requests are processed, and thus causing a certain downtime.

Each paradigm has its pros and cons, and its technical complexity. Choices should be adapted to the usage context.

SIZING & PERFORMANCE

In order to correctly set the technical architecture, we must also define server (or node) sizing through three main parameters: CPU, RAM and Disk Size (storage).

The main inputs to define this sizing are:

- ✓ What is the average message size (or request size)?
- ✓ What is the average number of requests (or calls) per unit of time?
- ✓ Are there any "peak events" to manage?
- ✓ What are the constraints on response time?

Performance testing is a good approach to confirm that a system is fit for purpose. To ensure meaningful results, the design of the performance test scenarios should be based on representative data sets in terms of size, date types, and frequency.

Intuitively, when implementing a new data integration layer, we want to look for the "best" in terms of performance. In real life, there is no such thing as "best" performance, and a thorough assessment should be performed to ensure you have the performance you need.

Performance is determined by several factors:

- ✓ **Tool** related: Some factors are intrinsically related to the solution you are employing, such as its development language, algorithms efficiency or libraries used.
- ✓ **Use case** related: performance is also affected by the use cases you are implementing: web services do not require the same performance as batch processing. It also depends on your data volumes and business requirements. High

frequency trading platforms on a major stock exchange do not have the same requirements as a business intelligence solution that is fed yearly with the company's financial results.

✓ **Technical architecture**: depending on your technical architecture choices, the same solution delivered on two different deployment configurations will not behave in the same manner. The results will differ if you deploy in one virtual machine with, for example, a 2 vCores CPU and 8 GB RAM against an active/active cluster of 8 virtual machines, each having 8 vCores and 64 GB RAM.

✓ **Network**: Data Integration aims at exchanging data, and depending on your network, you might face network latencies that cause your data flows to suffer. Network latency can be a challenge in hybrid integrations when you have applications in the cloud and others in your datacenter, or when you have to integrate applications from multiple datacenters that are geographically spread across many continents, and your data flows use massive amounts of data.

✓ **Backends and frontends performance**: In the data integration scenario, you have to interact with multiple applications to get or write data. Even with a performant tool, a performant network and a performant technical architecture, you may still encounter poor performance because of the capacity of the systems you interact with. An impact assessment should ideally be performed on each application to which the data integration layer will connect in order to project how these applications will perform and, in some cases, take proactive actions to optimize them for the upcoming integrations. Symmetrically, the data integration layer might impact the performance of the systems it is calling, especially transactional backend systems on which the data integration layer might be running heavy requests.

✓ **Algorithms:** when developing data integration flows, developers should produce efficient algorithms. Tool vendors will generally "sell" the idea that coding on the data integration layer is easy as you just need to use "arrows and boxes" and promote a low-code or no-code approach. This might be true for straightforward integrations or passthrough standard data flows, but as the data flow becomes more complex, specific skills are required to build high-performance integrations. When integrating with databases, using delta logic instead of full logic or relying on indexes instead of other columns can make a huge difference. When managing data transformation, adopting one algorithm or the other might make a difference as well.

Performance is generally considered mainly from the tool perspective, which is a mistake. Although tool performance is important, it is not often the main cause of poor performance. When assessing performance, a comprehensive picture of all factors should be considered.

In case of poor performance, a bottleneck analysis should be performed to determine which steps take the longest time and identify optimization levers for all the factors.

CLOUD DEPLOYMENT

New cloud architectures with major cloud providers like Amazon Web Services (AWS), Microsoft Azure, and Google Cloud Platform provide new features such as autoscaling groups, which enable dynamic resource allocation through scale up or scale down depending on the workload.

Automatic scaling will allow timely management and optimization of the resources (and hence the cost), with regards to the workload.

CHAPTER SEVEN
Data Integration Projects

In this book, I would like to introduce the DIPF, Data Integration Project Framework. DIPF is a new framework that I developed for this book (and for my courses). It aims at providing an actionable plan to help you build your Data Integration projects in a structured manner. It is a generic approach to adopt and adapt to your specific needs.

STEP #1: Why do you need Data Integration? Ask the right questions

The first step in a data integration setup project is to identify the business use cases: What are the business needs that might translate into a Data Integration need?

To do so, start by identifying your business contacts who may have Data Integration needs. Plan workshops to try to gather various business needs and demonstrate the capabilities of data integration tools to help your business contacts understand the technology and how it can match their needs. Moreover, you can organize brainstorming sessions to help business contacts better understand the "As-Is" situation and possible "To-be" solutions. To gain traction, find a "good sponsor" among your business contacts, preferably at the C-Level, such as a Chief Marketing Officer (CMO), a Chief Finance Officer (CFO) or a Chief Technology Officer (CTO). Sponsorship will be a key success factor in such a journey!

142

Following these sessions, qualify, formalize, and map the discussed business use cases. For each use case, clearly identify:

- ✓ Business domains in need of Data Integration: Sales, Supply Chain, Finance & Accounting, Customer Service, Marketing, Engineering...
- ✓ Pain points faced by the business: Data Quality, Data Freshness, Data Transfer, Data Monitoring, Data Governance...
- ✓ Value drivers expressed by the business, or in simple terms, the business benefits from implementing the expressed business data integration use case such as improving customer service efficiency, improving supply chain resilience, responding to regulatory constraints, etc.

Once you have established a consolidated view of the business use cases, proceed to qualify them by determining how the related business's problems are addressed today:

- ✓ Are there any solutions in place already?
  - o Any Point-to-Point integrations?
  - o Any Manual Data Transfer?
- ✓ Have there been any initiatives in the past aimed at addressing these use cases? If so, what is the current status, and what are the lessons learned so far?

Data Integration solution implementations are structuring projects that can be complex and costly. It is critical to start the journey only if there is a real business need and clearly identified business value.

Even if Data Integration projects are seen as technical in nature, its business part should be clear and consistent. It should not be conducted solely as an IT project, but rather with the necessary business involvement.

> 99
>
> *"Never implement a Data Integration Solution for the "pleasure" of implementing a technical solution. It should respond to a **real business need**, clearly identified, with **clear business value**."*

STEP #2: What use cases to address? Identify value & feasibility

Now that you have identified the business use cases and completed a first-level qualification of them, you will need to classify them by Business value: which use cases will bring the highest business value.

To keep it simple, you can ask the business stakeholders to assign a "mark" from 0 to 5 to each use case, with 5 being the most valuable.

Business value, however, cannot be the only criterion; it should be coupled with technical complexity. You can have very valuable use cases, but if their technical feasibility is highly complex or costly, implementing them may not be a smart idea.

Hence, you can ask the technical team (or technical experts, or even yourself if you have a technical background) to assign each use case a "mark" from 0 to 5, with 5 being the easiest to address.

Let's assume you collected 5 use cases, as follows:

Use case	Business Value	Technical feasibility
A	1	4
B	3	1
C	5	3
D	1	1
E	5	4

With a simple plot, we can visualize how this can help in the decision-making process:

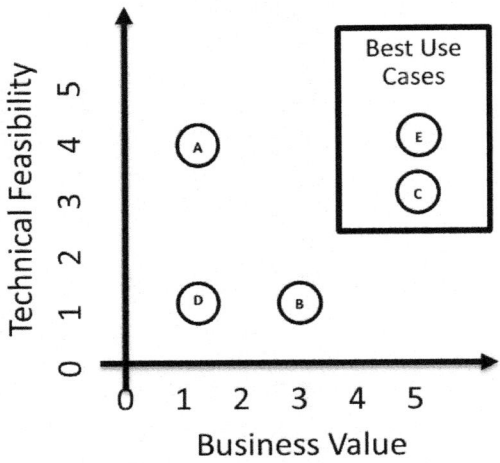

In this view, the use cases E and C seem to maximize business value, and to be "quick wins" as their technical feasibility is of low complexity. On the other hand, use case D has a low business value and a high level of technical complexity, making it the "worst" use case. Because use case A has a low level of complexity but also a low added value, it can be considered a "quick win" in the next step. Use case B has an average business value and a high level of technical complexity, making this use case not a great choice.

This view aims to visualize how the use cases rate on the two axes of business value and technical feasibility and assists in determining which use cases to prioritize in the Data integration setup project.

It is possible to add multiple other dimensions. There is no perfect evaluation matrix, and it will always be perceived as a simplification of the problem, potentially making the decision challengeable. It is, nevertheless, a powerful tool as it provides the right trade-off with a minimum of rationale and the least amount of complexity.

146

The following variables can be analyzed using the other dimensions that can be considered:

✓ *Lead time*: the shorter the lead time to deliver the use case, the better, so you might want to add it as an additional criterion. It can, however, be correlated to the technical feasibility dimension.

✓ *Risk of not doing*: this can be considered especially if you have some compliance or regulatory constraints like building a data integration with the local tax authority to transfer invoice data. Compliance or regulatory use cases might imply penalties or legal consequences if not completed and should therefore be taken with high priority.

✓ *Short-term vs. Long-term:* you might want to give more weight to use cases that have a long-term impact or that induce transformation against use cases that have an immediate impact but little long-term value.

Besides, every use case can be assigned a global score using a simple formula, an average or a weighted average: for example, you can consider business value as being twice as important as technical complexity. A possible score would be:

$$S = \frac{2 \times Business\ Value\ score + Technical\ complexity\ score}{3}$$

Regardless of the formula you use, make certain that:

✓ You do not overcomplicate the evaluation of use cases: keep the framework simple by setting a voting process with your business contacts (to vote for business value) and your technical team (to vote for technical feasibility).

✓ Never forget that business value should be a non-negotiable criterion.

✓ Provide feedback to your business contacts on what has been selected and what has not been with a clear rationale. The rest of the use cases might still be addressed at a later stage, or if their assessment changes over time or can be included as part of a mid-term or long-term roadmap.

✓ Maintain flexibility in your selection: if you have two complementary use cases, you can choose both of them instead of only one, or you can choose the use case that may not have the highest business value, but still has a certain level of value and is, for example, strongly sponsored. Sponsorship level can even be added as a dimension to the assessment.

STEP #3: Which solution for your first use case? The Solutions Panel

Hundreds of technical solutions are available to help you deliver a data integration use case.

It is recommended to identify a reasonable panel of solutions to evaluate from this huge number of possibilities, typically less than 10 solutions, with 5 serving as the "magic" number.

There will be some functional overlap among the considered solutions, but there will also be multiple differentiators that might or not be important for your use cases.

You should assess each solution based on major features you would like to use, such as supporting batch processing or the availability of specific connectors to your information system's applications.

The choice of the solution is based on more than just the capabilities of the solution. You do not need the one that costs the most or the one with the most connectors. The solution should be selected based on how well it meets your needs.

Moreover, at this step of the DIPF, the decisions you make might not be your final decisions: you will have to iterate on a first MVP (minimum viable product) which will help you gain maturity and, eventually, make better decisions.

There may be several solutions that satisfy your need for a first use case (the MVP), but only a few will fit your overall need, which includes all of your use cases. Thus, when evaluating market solutions, make sure that you consider your options from a "full perspective", taking into account all of the use cases that your organization requires or may require now and in the future.

Building such a consolidated view is not an easy task, and it requires alignment with the business on their roadmaps.

To define the solution panel to evaluate, you can think of solutions you know, solutions you heard positive user feedback about, or solutions you have used in the past. You can also include solutions that have been recommended by your peers or colleagues. It is also advisable to investigate what your competitors are using, especially if they are in the same industry and with comparable size. Another option is to check reviews and websites like Gartner, Forrester, Capterra or G2, where you can find valuable inputs, examples, and user feedback to aid in your research.

You can consider some exclusion criteria to help you evaluate only the solution that might be a good fit.

For example, you might choose to exclude all proprietary solutions and only consider Open Source, or you might want to consider only solutions that have a specific feature or connector. Pricing is another important limiting factor, and you may want to exclude any solutions that do not fit within your budget.

After receiving initial feedback and excluding those that do not meet your major criteria, you should have your final solutions panel of 5 or close to 5 solutions at this point. This solutions panel should now be evaluated.

The evaluation of the solutions panel should be based on clear and tangible criteria. These criteria should cover:

- ✓ The features offered by the solution, and which ones are must-have or nice-to-have for the expected use cases:
    - ○ Supported patterns: ETL, ESB, EDI…
    - ○ Connectors: ERP, SaaS, Web services…
- ✓ Data Transformation
- ✓ Technical architecture
- ✓ Deployment options: on-prem, private cloud, SaaS…
- ✓ Security: encryption, authentication mechanisms…
- ✓ Performance: parallelization, message size…
- ✓ Operations management
- ✓ Pricing and licensing model

Each assessment criteria should be associated with a weight.

Here is an example of what your assessment can look like:

Domain	Criteria	Weight	Solution A	Solution B	Solution C
Feature	ETL capability	40	40	40	0
Feature	Connector to DB X	30	0	30	30
Feature	Connector to ERP Y	30	0	30	0
Feature	SOAP connector	25	25	0	25
Performance	Handle 50 messages/s	50	50	45	20
Deployment	Private Cloud A support	25	25	25	0
Security	OAuth 2.0 support	50	0	50	0
…					
Total		250	140/250	220/250	75/250

According to this assessment, solution B seems to be the best option for the next steps. Solution B does not "check all the boxes" but has the highest score.

It is important to note that for some criteria, it can be "full score or nothing" like the presence of a connector, whereas for other criteria, it can be different like performance, where a normalized measurement can be considered.

In real assessments, tables can reach up to 200 criteria. I have included a longer list of criteria below so you can use it to help with your assessment.

CONNECTORS

Keep only the connectors that are relevant to your context:

- ✓ Relational Databases
- ✓ NOSQL databases
- ✓ REST Webservices
- ✓ SOAP Webservices
- ✓ OData
- ✓ Delimited-text data (like CSV)
- ✓ Fixed-width files
- ✓ XML files
- ✓ JSON files
- ✓ Spreadsheets (and Excel files)
- ✓ Data storage
- ✓ File Transfer
- ✓ CDC
- ✓ Messaging
- ✓ AS2
- ✓ LDAP
- ✓ GraphQL
- ✓ SaaS applications you are using or planning to use

✓ Specific connectors for specific data types (Audio, Video, Emails, rich media, etc.)
✓ Add any other connectors or specific applications that you use or intend to use in your information system

You can put higher weights for connectors that will be used for multiple applications (typically for your ERP, databases and Web services connectors). You can also choose lower weights for low priority connectors or connectors for which you are unsure whether or not you will use them in the target roadmap.

INTEGRATION PATTERNS AND ARCHITECTURE

The following criteria can be assessed:

✓ Batch scheduling and processing
✓ Exposing new interfaces and APIs
✓ Supporting SOA
✓ Supporting Services Orchestration and multi-step processes
✓ Supporting conditional transitions and looping
✓ Supporting throttling
✓ Supporting dynamic routing and multicast

DATA TRANSFORMATION

The following data transformation criteria can be assessed:

✓ Simple data transformation, such as data type conversions, simple string operations, simple calculations, or data format conversions
✓ Intermediate data transformation such as lookup operations, aggregations and sets operations, or deterministic matching

- ✓ Complex data transformation like probabilistic matching or XSLT transformation
- ✓ Custom data transformation through supporting developing custom scripts
- ✓ You should also make a list of any specific transformations you might need, such as CSV to Excel, XML to JSON, or any other that your use cases might require.

SECURITY

Security criteria can cover:

- ✓ Data encryption
- ✓ Support of authentication mechanisms
- ✓ Support of authorization mechanisms
- ✓ User management
- ✓ Support MFA, Multi-factor authentication, for users' access
- ✓ Protection against DoS (Denial of Service) or DDoS (Distributed Denial of Service) attacks for the data integration layer exposing web services
- ✓ Protection against SQL Injection attacks if the data integration layer connects to relational databases
- ✓ Providing RBAC (Role Based Access Control)
- ✓ Integration with IAM (Identity Access Management) tools
- ✓ Data masking, tokenization, or anonymization

HIGH AVAILABILITY AND RESILIENCE

This set of criteria should address the system's ability to perform expected computations and recover from failures. Criteria can include the following:

- ✓ High availability (active/active or active/passive), with a target availability > 99,99% (or your target availability)
- ✓ Data integrity
- ✓ Capacity of recovery from crashes and major failures
- ✓ Data loss prevention
- ✓ Backup and recovery
- ✓ Virtualization (supporting deployment on virtual machines)
- ✓ Cloud deployment
- ✓ Horizontal and/or vertical scalability
- ✓ Supporting geo-redundancy and disaster recovery architectures
- ✓ Supporting the needed performance

Performance requirements should be expressed with regards to the planned use cases. Some solutions may perform well with the ESB pattern but not with the ETL pattern. Estimations of the expected number of daily transactions or data records, the average volume of the messages, the expected response time, as well as the forecast of expected growth in the coming years should all help frame the expected target performance.

OPERATIONS MANAGEMENT

The selected data integration tool should be able to provide a set of features that enable efficient operations management during run time. Criteria in this domain can include:

- ✓ Monitoring and supervision
- ✓ Exception management and error handling
- ✓ Runtime analytics
- ✓ Logging
- ✓ Security alerts

- ✓ Resource consumption threshold notifications
- ✓ Auditing trails
- ✓ CI/CD and deployment automation
- ✓ Supporting "hot" (or zero downtime) deployments
- ✓ Administration tooling
- ✓ Automatic and configurable retry mechanisms

LICENSING OPTIONS

In the assessment criteria, it is possible to include licensing criteria. When choosing a data integration solution, you might want to limit yourself to free solutions, open-source solutions, solutions providing perpetual licensing, or subscription models. For subscription models, multiple metrics can be used to determine the pricing, such as the number of transactions, the volume of data processes, or the number of CPUs.

OTHER REQUIREMENTS

Depending on your needs, you might want to add more requirements such as:

- ✓ Data Tagging
- ✓ Metadata management
- ✓ Master Data Management capabilities
- ✓ Data Governance capabilities
- ✓ Integrated code repository with version control capability
- ✓ Data streaming
- ✓ Specific needs for graphical user interfaces
- ✓ Data quality rules definition
- ✓ Data lineage

✓ Interfaces automatic documentation generation
✓ Data export and data dump
✓ Transaction management (and rollback management)

WRAP UP

At the end of this step, you should have a clearly defined panel, which has been assessed against the criteria that you have chosen and are relevant to your use cases.

STEP #4: How to implement your first use case? The MVP

So far, we have identified the "right" use case as well as the "right" solution to address it. So, what comes next?

The following step is to build your MVP.

MVP stands for Minimum Viable Product. You can check "The Lean Startup" by Eric Ries if you would like to delve deeper into this notion (recommended reading, even if not directly related to data integration).

The MVP should be "small enough" in order to secure its delivery and "big enough" to ensure significance. The MVP should also help you obtain initial feedback to iterate. It should also aid in the direction of technical and functional decisions.

MVP BUILD MODEL

Now that you have the "What" (Use Case) and the "Why" (Business value), you need to define the "How" in order to build your MVP: How will you develop and deploy your MVP?

You can consider a variety of options based on your situation; you can depend on yourself if you are starting your own startup, your team, or maybe another team in your organization. You can also consider one of your IT service suppliers or your software vendor's professional services team.

Consider the following variables and criteria as part of your decision-making process:

✓ *Do you have any budget?* If yes, collaborating with a partner like your IT services supplier is a smart alternative in this scenario because it will "validate" a possible delivery model: indeed, once you deploy the solution, your IT services supplier can provide you with build and development services for your new needs

✓ *Did you try to negotiate with the software vendor?* Try negotiating a "free" MVP / POC (Proof of Concept) with the editor. Some software editors might accept to do it for free! This is more likely to work if you negotiate with a proprietary solution vendor that you have put in competition.

✓ *Do you have skilled in-house developers who are knowledgeable about the tool to be used?* If yes, this can be a good option. I have seen in some organizations that even the choice of the tool is conditioned by the presence of skilled developers who master the tool in the organization.

✓ *Else, what can I do?* You can still have training (you or a member of your team) and develop the MVP yourself, which has many benefits: you will gain a better understanding of the tool "from the inside" and will be able to better capitalize on related knowledge internally. Self-paced training is generally available for free by software vendors.

MVP PLANNING

Now that the delivery model is defined, the MVP should be planned.

In this process, you need to decide your methodology from a project delivery perspective.

You should also specify some technical choices, such as the technical architecture, the deployment configuration (for example, will you implement in a private cloud or in your data center), and to which applications you will connect. You should also set up governance processes, such as Steering Committees with key stakeholders for decision-making, as well as follow-up and Operational Committees to drive the project.

During the MVP execution, you can still adjust some elements and details: you can adapt the planning and the use case scope, typically simplifying it if it seems too complex or starts to take too long.

An MVP can also follow the "Try and trash" way: You are in iterative mode, and if the MVP is not successful, you can return to Step #1 after taking a step back and identifying the failure reason(s): Too high expectations? The solution is not suitable? The use case is too complex? The priorities have evolved?

Once your MVP is executed, you should be able to validate it and confirm that it is fit for use based on the success criteria you have pre-identified.

STEP #5: How to move to the next step? The Industrialization Plan

Once you have validated your MVP, you should prepare how you will "industrialize" it. Industrialization entails transitioning from a prototyping phase, where the level of uncertainty is quite high and the level of maturity is quite low, to a maturity phase, where the level of uncertainty has decreased. In short, you are more certain that:

- ✓ Use case: you have a use case that has validated the business value.
- ✓ Technical solution: you have selected a technical solution to serve as a data integration layer that responds to your needs and information system's constraints.
- ✓ Delivery model: you are able to establish a delivery model to deliver your use cases, which may require adjustments when industrializing.
- ✓ Key learnings: you have lessons learned from the MVP experiment that should be addressed in order to get the industrialization phase off to a good start.

The industrialization plan should include the steps to finalize the selection of the tool, as well as any related "options" like add-ons, customizations, or specific modules. It should also cover a detailed plan on your project delivery, including your budget, planning, and delivery model. Finally, it should state how you intend to maintain your tool implementation over time and once the setup project is successfully delivered.

Your industrialization plan should contain this full view and actionable and detailed steps. It will be your roadmap, and it must be shared and agreed upon by all of your stakeholders.

STEP #6: The final choices

Step#6 is about making the big decisions for your project: the tool selection and the project methodology

---

STEP #6.1: HOW TO SELECT THE TARGET TOOL? THE SOLUTION

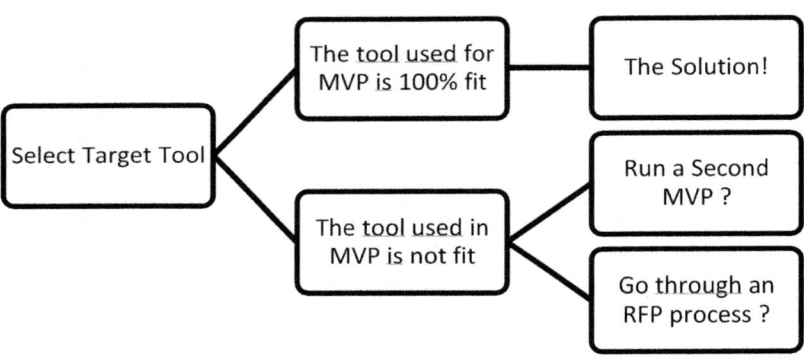

In order to finalize the choice of the target tool, you need to rely first on the conclusions from the MVP. If you consider your MVP as conclusive based on the tool's capabilities, you can move forward with it. Otherwise, you could run a second MVP, or you can think of launching an RFP (Request for Proposals) to the software vendors you are considering. Both approaches have pros and cons. An MVP should produce better results in general, but it can be costly and take considerable effort. An RFP process might be an alternative if you have a very specific idea on what you are looking for, but it can also take a long time to complete. You must weigh both scenarios with the goal of selecting the best solutions for your business use cases. Consultation and alignment with business counterparts can also help you decide which path to take, and business counterpart buy-in is mandatory to avoid any frustrations associated with long lead times to select your tool.

The data integration tool you select should be aligned with your requirements, as presented in Step #3, following a complete 360° assessment.

STEP #6.2: HOW TO DELIVER YOUR PROJECT? THE PROJECT METHODOLOGY

Choosing the right project methodology can be a real accelerator to your project. Multiple project methodologies might suit your needs, and there is no "one-size-fits-all" methodology.

This book is not intended to present a comprehensive overview of project methodologies. There are many books and courses that provide a thorough understanding of this topic. This course will only provide you with "hints" to help you make better decisions in case you are starting a new Data Integration project. Hence, we will focus here on the most common methodologies shared in a simplified manner. But, there are a lot of variants that you can consult to fine-tune your strategy so you can lead your project to achieve your business goals while respecting your constraints (timeline, budget, etc.)

To provide you with some examples of project methodologies, we will briefly discuss two main approaches: V-Model and Agile.

The V-Model approach will start by fully defining your requirements and architecture, followed by a detailed design before launching the implementation phase. After implementation, test and integration will begin, leading to the operations phase as presented in this simplified schema

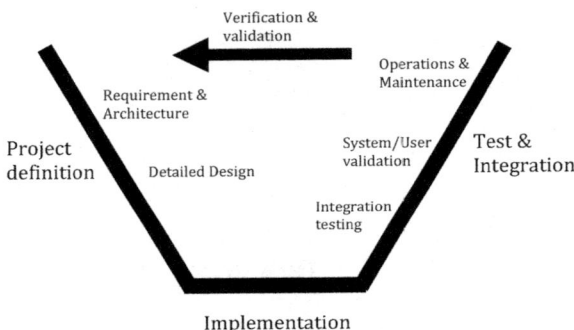

Implementation

The V-Model is appropriate if all your requirements are clear (and ideally, frozen) upfront. You also need to prepare the testing scenarios at an early stage.

This methodology minimizes total risk with a frozen design at the end of the project's definition phase.

It is the conventional and classic approach. Any change must go through a change request process, during which the change is studied, defined, designed and its impact analysis reviewed before being implemented. From this perspective, as well as from the perspective of requiring a fully detailed design upfront, this approach has a certain level of rigidity.

On the other hand, Agile and Scrum methodologies may be more appropriate in a "changing environment" situation.

Agile is based on building intermediate increments of your solution defined by sprints. Sprints are derived from your product's global backlog, including all of the features (and user stories) that need to be built. The following simplified schema provides a quick overview of this methodology.

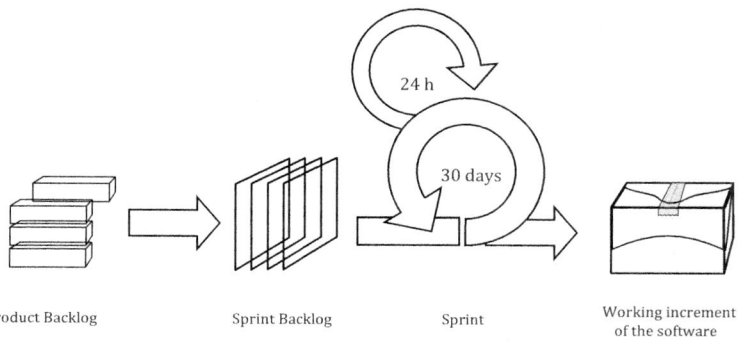

Product Backlog   Sprint Backlog   Sprint   Working increment of the software

This methodology helps to avoid the "tunnel effect" that the V-Model might create through the use of an iterative approach. It can be useful (and powerful) when working on projects that consist of multiple independent data flows, to consider each as an increment, for example.

The agile methodology is gaining more and more traction and becoming more mature and widely adopted.

Regardless of the methodology chosen and again, the two presented examples are just high-level examples, as this book is not intended to be a project management guide, your decision-making process should be based on a pragmatic choice depending on the maturity of your requirements as well as the maturity of your organization to go with the chosen approach.

STEP #7: Project execution

Now you are all set! You have developed a clear business use case with significant added value, identified your key stakeholders, selected your tool and project methodology, and elaborated a clear timeboxed planning.

You can move now to the project execution. Only at this seventh step does the project execution begin. This is a major pillar in the DIPF approach. In many cases, project execution starts right away without any prior due diligence. This could lead to a poor solution choice and/or project execution, resulting in project failure and a frustrating environment for business stakeholders.

To succeed in project execution, you need to master your project planning by applying the selected project methodology. All project methodologies, whether V-Model, Agile, or any other methodology, will aim to meet committed deadlines if the requirements and dependencies are met.

Before launching the project and during project execution, ensure that your risks are identified and anticipated, with clear mitigation plans in place, and that the risks are communicated to your business stakeholders, teams, and partners in a transparent manner.

In addition, make sure you have efficient "governance instances": Operational Committees (generally intended to take operational decisions for day-to-day project operations) and Steering Committees (generally intended to give steer and take major decisions like arbitrations on scope, on tool choice,...) that are empowered to make needed decisions and arbitrations.

During project execution, tunnel effects should be avoided, even if you chose a V-Model approach, by organizing demos and incorporating stakeholder feedback.

Your project will have multiple important milestones, such as the end of the design phase or the end of the implementation phase for V-Model, or milestones related to backlog finalization and milestones related to major product increments for Agile. But, regardless of the methodology you choose, you must reach the critical "Go Live" or "Move to production" milestone for your project, after which it materializes and starts to be used in real business conditions, and hence starts to generate value.

Only proceed with this milestone if your deliverables have undergone thorough testing. Although it seems obvious, this step is sometimes neglected, which might lead to disastrous consequences afterwards.

Besides, make sure that you have prepared a clear and controlled cut-over plan with strict checkpoints and roll-back scenarios to mitigate risks in case things don't go as planned.

Because there will be other applications and dependencies, particularly in Data Integration projects, high coordination should be ensured: your data integration layer will connect to multiple applications, and your plan should cover these dependencies by working collaboratively with the various teams managing those applications.

Make certain to organize the support phase post-go-live as well, as business users will start having data flow on the data integration layer and will need a "facing" team to assist them with any issues they may encounter when using the new tool.

Last but not least, do not forget about communication! It's an important milestone! Communication should ensure factual information sharing with all stakeholders, clarifying what is changing and in which manner to ensure adoption, and highlighting and valorizing the achieved results!

STEP #8: Transition to "Operations"

Once the project is delivered, your data integration layer will be used in real-world scenarios by your business. Thus, a dedicated new stream should be set up to manage the operations of this new phase.

"Operations", also referred to as "Run" or "Support" is responsible for keeping your Data Integration Layer operational, assisting users and managing incidents.

Operations should be structured outside of the project. Unlike a project with a start date and an end date, Operations are a continuous activity. Operations can, however, feed future projects on Data Integration by providing a continuous feedback and improvement loop.

CHAPTER EIGHT
Operations Management

Operations Management Model

Once the project "Go live" is reached, and the new Data Integration tool setup is being used for business operations, an Operations Management Model (or Support Model or Run Model) should be defined.

This should cover the "make or buy equation" in particular. Many organizations believe that such an activity is not part of their core business model and should thus be outsourced; however, others believe that this activity is critical enough to be internalized. The model should specify who is in charge of this activity. It is also worth noting that new SaaS models, particularly EIPaaS (Enterprise Integration Platform as a Service) can provide a tool with its operations management model as a software vendor offering, taking in charge the platform hosting, generally via a cloud offering, as well as the operations management of the platform. This, however, will certainly add a certain cost that should be estimated and provisioned.

The operations management model should also clarify how to operationalize supervision activities on the platform, monitor data flows, and manage notifications, specifying who and when to notify about certain warnings or incidents on the platform.

Moreover, it should address Incident management topics, clarifying the processes and the SLA (Service Level Agreement).

Access management and access governance are also critical topics in the Operations Management Model for ensuring legitimate access and avoiding security breaches through unauthorized or malicious access.

Vendor Support

Depending on the tool chosen, you may have access to Software Vendor support.

For some Open-source solutions, you generally have access to the community portal, forum, or knowledge database, and in some cases, paid support packages can be offered, providing a higher support level than simply accessing community material.

Support packages for commercial solutions, on the other hand, are subject to additional fees and they provide you with privileged access to the software support team. The budget to consider for this support is generally around 20% of your contract value. It can be a little lower for basic support and much higher, up to 50% in some cases, for premium packages with aggressive SLA.

Vendor support generally provides you with access to the latest software version (upgrades), as well as fixes and security patches, ensuring that the tool setup is secure and up to date.

Monitoring and Alerts

Monitoring is a critical activity of Support management. It consists in continuously monitoring the system, whether manually or automatically, in order to identify various issues, incidents, or warnings that might trigger incidents.

To assure efficient monitoring, critical thresholds that should trigger alerts should be identified, such as CPU usage reaching 90%, RAM usage reaching 80%, or Disk space usage reaching 75%.

Once an alert is detected, it should be routed through a timely and reliable communication channel like Emails or SMS, as well as a ticketing, or ITSM (IT Management System tool), such as Service Now, HP Service Manager, or BMC Remedy for example, in order to reach knowledgeable contacts that can assist in resolution and track the resolution status, along with, if applicable, business contacts or key users whose activity may have been impacted by this ongoing issue.

Continuous monitoring is essential in Data Integration to make sure that data flows are executed accurately and at the right performance level. Many tools can help automate monitoring, spanning from built-in monitoring capabilities within the data integration tool to dedicated APM, or Application Performance Monitoring solutions, such as Splunk, Dynatrace or Nagios, or generic solutions like RPA (Robotic Process Automation) that can mimic human monitoring, such as Automation Anywhere, UiPath or Blueprism.

Incidents' Management

To manage incidents, an end-to-end process that clarifies actors and stakeholders, as well as the activities to be performed to bring the incident to resolution should be defined and adopted.

You should also clearly categorize incident priority; for example, a Priority 1 incident in case the platform is totally down, or a Priority 3 incident in case the impact is limited to 1 out of 1000 non-business-critical transactions failing. The process may differ depending on the priority, as not all incidents have the same impact and require the same level of response.

For efficient incident management and for the sake of clarity, it is critical to define the SLA (Service Level Agreement) with your business to set resolution target timelines aligned with business priorities and outcomes. SLA can also be defined with your external support team if you have opted for an outsource model, as well as with the tool vendor if you have a specific contract for tool-related issues.

Overtime, KPI (Key Performance Indicators) tracking will help measure performance of operations like the percentage of compliance with SLA, LTTR (Lead Time To Resolve), MTBF (Mean Time Between Failures), etc.

Communication is also crucial when managing incidents. Useful communication should be sent to the right stakeholders to inform them of the platform's status and provide regular updates, especially on critical incidents.

Let's take a look at this use case from Happy Tel as an example.

Happy Tel manages users' subscriptions via the data integration layer. Users can subscribe to new services directly from the mobile application. The Data Integration layer is used between the mobile application (Front-End) and the provisioning service (Back-End).

Let's assume that Happy Tel's mobile application serves around 20 million customers. New subscriptions made through the application generate an average of 20.000 US$ per hour.

Because the Data Integration layer is down, the data flow is currently disrupted, and users can no longer subscribe to new services.

The SLA Matrix used in Happy Tel is as follows:

Incident Type	Impact Definition	SLA Resolution
Priority 1	A critical feature is unavailable to more than **1M subscribers** affecting **revenues** and **brand image**, or posing a high **security** breach risk	< 2 hours
Priority 2	A critical or major feature is unavailable to less than 1M and more than 10.000 **subscribers,** with limited impact on **revenues**, **brand image** or security	< 4 hours
Priority 3	A major or minor feature is unavailable to less than 10.000 subscribers, with relatively limited impact	< 24 hours

As per this matrix, the incident is considered Priority 1, with 20M subscribers impacted and high revenue loss.

The Operations team should resolve the issue in less than 2 hours according to the SLA.

On the other hand, if an incident occurs, for example, and results in the user profile not loading in full on the mobile application and only affects a small number of users, such as 100, the incident will be considered as Priority 3 and the Operations team will have up to 24 hours to fix it.

Environment Maintenance

SCHEDULED MAINTENANCE

Scheduled maintenance is a set of operations that must be performed in a given environment. It is generally planned upfront to perform patches, fixes, security updates, software upgrades, or new deployments.

Once a scheduled maintenance is identified and planned, relevant stakeholders should be notified, especially if an action, such as running a certain testing or sanity check, is required on their end, or if the system might experience downtime. Communication should provide clear information on the planned maintenance's date and time, scope, estimated impacts, and whether the recipient needs to take any action.

In a highly available environment, such maintenance should ideally be performed without any downtime. Hot deployment options might exist to manage maintenance activities while the system is running, with no downtime of services and data flows.

In an Active/Active environment, it is possible to manage maintenance activities without causing service disruption. In this case, it is recommended to manage maintenance on each active node separately. Before launching the maintenance activities, the node to be maintained should be "isolated" or "disconnected" from the group, go through maintenance, and then be reinserted into the group.

In an Active/Passive environment, it is also generally possible to manage such activities without downtime. The approach entails managing maintenance on all standby nodes before moving on to the "active" node. Before launching the activities on the "active" node, it should be stopped, and data flows should be processed by a standby node on which maintenance activities have previously been performed.

ENVIRONMENT'S CLEANUP

As the usage of the data integration layer increases, it is necessary to keep your environments "clean".

First, for security purposes and user management, ensure that you have proper user definition and access. Typically, you must verify that users who are no longer a part of the team or the company are deactivated. You must also ensure that roles are defined for the various profiles you have, such as developers, support team, architects, or external support team. New data integration tools usually include RBAC (Role Based Access Control) features that allow for fine-grained control over who can access what.

Then, old installation files must be removed because they might get executed accidently, they might contain some vulnerabilities that could harm your information system, and they consume disk space.

It is also important to remove old log files and other monitoring and regularly created files like old cache files, while processing. Such operations should be done in accordance with a predefined retention policy, especially for log files, and offline and cold archiving can be a viable alternative.

All of these operations are often performed without affecting existing data flows.

CHAPTER NINE
A quick overview of market solutions

Solution Components

A data integration tool is comprised of multiple components that address various needs and are targeted at different user profiles, in particular, developers and operations teams.

These components differ from one vendor (or solution) to another. The following sections will provide you with an overview of such components.

COMPONENTS FOR DEVELOPERS

The Business Process Modeling tool or interface is used by developers to model data flows. This component is sometimes referred to as "Studio".

The SDK, or Software Development Kit is used to create add-ons and connectors that are not available "out-of-the-box" in the tool.

The Data Mapping and Transformation Tool is used to model the data, its transformations and mapping between source and target models. This component can be embedded in the Studio (or the business process modeling tool).

The Connectors (or Adapters) library (or Palette) is used to define the connection to be built. The connectors library is generally extensible, and it is possible to import other connectors, either provided by the vendor, by the developer community in the case of an open source tool, or developed through the SDK.

The versioning tool is used to "commit" code modifications and keep track of various versions as the project progresses. Versioning is useful in the case of code loss, damage to live environments, or the need to revert to a previous version if subsequent versions have caused some incidents.

COMPONENTS FOR OPERATIONS TEAM

The Administration Console (Graphical user interface) is used by the operations team to check the status of current deployments and launch new deployments once new data integrations are planned for roll out.

The Administration command line tool is used by operations for a scope comparable to that of the administration console, but it is available through command line. This can be the case because no graphical user interface is accessible or can be used to automate deployments in a DevOps approach. Building CI/CD (Continuous Integration / Continuous Deployment) pipelines for deploying data flows has a number of advantages, including accelerating time to market, ensuring shorter deployment lead times, and removing human error by introducing automations. In this case, the administration command line tool is called by the tool managing the CI/CD pipeline, such as Puppet, Chef, or Jenkins, rather than by the operations team.

The Monitoring Dashboard tool is a component that is increasingly being added to new tools to assist the operations team in obtaining information about the system's running data flows as well as some performance metrics. The scope covered by this dashboard varies depending on the tool architecture and the capabilities implemented by each vendor. It is, in some cases, included in the Administration Console tool.

The License Consumption Monitoring tool is provided by software vendors to monitor the metrics that are used to license the software. For example, some data integration tools are licensed based on the number of CPUs or transactions. The license consumption monitoring tool will provide a view of these metrics and whether the usage is in compliance with the license terms. It might, in some situations, send alerts to the Vendor to warn them about a non-authorized use. In other instances, it might totally block non-authorized use of the tool, or it can simply be there for information purposes or for use by internal or external compliance audit teams. The license consumption monitoring tool is sometimes integrated within the Administration Console.

Open source vs Proprietary

We can group Data Integration market solutions into two main groups: Open source and Proprietary.

A quick disclaimer for the sake of clarity: this book and its author are not affiliated with any software vendor.

When working on a limited budget, Open source solutions can be a great option, especially for small and medium size businesses, minor projects, or some Proof of Concepts for illustration or testing purposes.

Some Open source solutions are really powerful and enterprise-grade, but you must do your own research to properly assess them. The size of the community and its level of involvement are major determinants, as are the frequency of new releases and the roadmap execution.

Open source solutions, however, are not always free for enterprise use, and community editions are increasingly becoming quite poor compared to a commercial offering based on the same core, to which the software vendor will add critical capabilities.

It is also a common misconception that open source means free. This is not always the case, and depending on the licensing metrics, some open source solutions can sometimes be even (much) more expensive than proprietary ones. However, direct access to the code can help you build specific customizations if required, as well as participate while also benefiting from community efforts to evolve the tool.

Proprietary solutions, on the other hand, are built exclusively for commercial use. There may be some trial or freemium models available, but with limited features and/or for a limited time.

Pricing for proprietary solutions will be based on a licensing model, and you must forecast your needs in order to negotiate a price that is suitable for you.

Hundreds of open source and proprietary solutions are available on the market. There is no generic recommendation to go for one over the other, and the main recommendation is to assess against your needs and constraints.

Examples of open source solutions include Talend, WSO2, OpenESB, Hitachi Vantara, Jitsu or Airbyte.

Examples of proprietary solutions include Tibco Business Works, Boomi, Microsoft Biztalk, IBM Websphere or Informatica or Fivetran.

Licensing, Pricing Models & TCO

In software licensing, we can distinguish two major models:

Perpetual licensing (sometimes referred to as CAPEX, or Capital Expense, as it is considered as an "investment"), in which the licensee has access to the tool without time limitation. However, other limitations might exist, such as the number of CPUs, the number of transactions, or any other metric that is not time bound.

Subscription licensing (also known as OPEX, or Operational Expense), in which the licensee has access to the tool for a limited period of time (generally one year, but sometimes 2 or 3 years, or n months). Other restrictions may apply, such as the number of CPUs, the number of transactions, or any other licensing metrics.

On top of the license cost, you generally need to pay the vendor around 20% - 25% of your license price each year to access upgrades, patches, security fixes, etc....

The cost of a license can range from 0 to several million dollars. To provide an order of magnitude, a proprietary solution used by a small or medium-sized business (SME) would cost between 20 000 and 50 000 dollars. For big corporations, it would cost from 200 000 to 5M dollars.

These numbers can vary greatly. A big corporation using a data integration tool for a small number of integrations and low adoption may pay as little as 10 000 dollars, whereas an SME employing a real-time data integration tool to manage a critical API with millions of transactions daily may pay hundreds of thousands of dollars. Again, this is just to give you an idea and provide some order of magnitude to keep in mind while benchmarking, and remember that prices will vary depending on the solution, your needs, and licensing metrics.

The licensing metrics used by software vendors are also quite different. Here are some examples:

- ✓ CPUs: the price is determined by the number of CPUs on the server (or virtual machine, or cloud instance) on which the software is installed. The number of CPUs necessary is usually proportional to the amount of processing power required, so the more processing power you require, the more you pay the software vendor
- ✓ Number of nodes: the price depends on the number of nodes on which you have installed the software. In the case of a high-availability setup and especially horizontal scalability, the price rises as you use more nodes.
- ✓ Number of transactions or records processed: this is more of a "pay-per-use" model, where you pay a fee for every transaction or record processed. The transaction metric can be used for ESB (and API), and EDI patterns, whereas the record metric is more applicable to ETL patterns.
- ✓ Volume of data exchanged: in this model, you pay a fee for every GB of data exchanged; it is mostly used in ETL and ELT patterns solutions, but also in some ESB ones.
- ✓ KC (or Kilo Character): this metric is very specific to EDI and is comparable to the volume of data exchanged.

Data integration solutions can significantly increase your TCO, or Total Cost of Ownership, even if they provide real value and there is generally a positive business case to implement such solutions, as they help improve lead times, increase business readiness, reduce time to market and remove long manual data transfer activities.

In order to compute a global TCO for your solution, you should include the license cost, vendor support cost, hosting cost, and team cost, whether internal or external.

As example, let's see how much the implementation of a Data Integration layer costs for Happy Tel:

License: Happy Tel chose a subscription model based on the volume of Data Exchanged. The cost per exchanged GB is $65, and the yearly volume exchanged is 2 TB.

$$C_L = Volume\ of\ data\ \times Unit\ cost = 2048\ \times 65 = \$133,120$$

Vendor Support: Happy Tel subscribed to a premium support package at a cost of 25% of the global yearly license price.

$$C_S = C_L \times Support\ Factor = 133,120 \times 0.25 = \$33,280$$

Hosting: In order to host the Data Integration solution, 5 cloud instances are used; 3 are for "lower environments" or "non-production" environments, which are employed for development, tests and pre-production, and 2 are for "production" environments, with a high availability setup. Each non-production instance costs $500 monthly, and each production instance costs $1000 monthly.

$$C_H = C_{non-prod} + C_{Prod} = (500 \times 3 + 1000 \times 2) \times 12 = \$42,000$$

Team Cost: To operate the solution, Happy Tel has 2 full-time team members, one Senior with an annual salary of $80,000 and one Junior with an annual salary of $50,000.

$$C_T = \sum_{Team\ member\ i} C_{T_i} = 80,000 + 50,000 = \$130,000$$

This, gives us a TCO, (Total Cost of ownership) of:

$$TCO = C_L + C_S + C_H + C_T = \$338,400$$

This example from Happy Tel provides a simplified view, as TCO might be difficult to compute. In fact, the following "complexities" have been left out of the example:

- The license cost didn't include a growth factor. As your business grows, so will the volume of data, and estimations at the end of the year might be higher than those at the beginning, and an increase in the volume of data might be included in the cost. In addition, we used a subscription model, whereas perpetual license calculations might be more difficult to compute as they depend on the accounting processes your organization applies in terms of CAPEX licenses amortizations. In the case of a perpetual license, it is common to include 1/5th of the total license cost in the TCO, which is equivalent to the amortization factor, but this is dependent on a number of other factors, such as internal accounting standards and country-specific accounting processes.
- Vendor support didn't include extra costs like professional services, or additional services. Depending on your situation, you may require additional vendor support that is not included in the support package.
- Hosting cost calculation might include other variables, such as temporary environment upscaling or shutdown of non-production environments when they are not in use. When it comes to cloud deployment, you have multiple options for optimizing the usage of the environments, and the FinOps discipline can help you manage these optimizations to

reduce your hosting cost while improving system performance.

- The team's cost didn't include any external support. It is possible that you will need external support, either on need basis or on a regular basis. Besides, you may have shared teams that provide support not only for the data integration tool but also for other tools in your information system, in which case, you only need to include a portion of their cost corresponding to the percentage of hours from their total number of working hours in the TCO. This team's cost also didn't include any development costs. We made the implicit assumption that development (Build) is done as part of dedicated projects with costs that are not tracked within the TCO.

CHAPTER TEN
Digital Transformation

Introduction

Digital Transformation is about implementing digital capabilities to support business processes in order to improve business outcomes.

Sales growth, higher value delivered to customers, reduced time to market, enhanced products, optimized business processes or cost avoidance are examples of business outcomes.

Data Integration and Data in general are key pillars in digital transformation, as they ensure that the right data is delivered to the right system or user at the right time, enabling digital transformation to take place by complementing its digital capabilities stack.

Data-driven Company Enabler

Data-driven companies make decisions based on accurate data analysis.

Data-driven companies have demonstrated overall better and quicker decision-making, as well as improved business outcomes.

Bringing data to business applications and data analytics tools in a timely and accurate manner, through a secure and performant data integration layer is critical to achieving this goal.

Data Science, AI and Predictive

Artificial Intelligence and Machine learning use cases support interesting predictive use cases, such as sales forecast, customer churn detection, fraud detection, recommendations, or predicting customer behavior.

In order to enable these use cases, accurate data should be provided through data integration layers from back-end systems like ERP and CRM to Data Science and AI/ML tools. In this regard, data integration plays a major and central role in enabling such usages.

Let's take an example from Happy Tel for churn detection. The purpose of the use case is to predict which subscribers will switch telecommunication operators and move from Happy Tel to one of their competitors.

To calculate a "churn score", a predictive data model is built based on subscriber usage, calls to customer support, satisfaction survey results and other customer information and interactions data.

The Data Integration layer will play a key role. It will provide a data pipeline to transport data from back-end systems (CRM, survey system...) to the predictive algorithm.

This will help reach the intended business outcome by identifying customers at high churn risk and taking necessary actions like calling them and suggesting commercial measures to retain them and avoid losing subscribers to competition.

IOT Use Cases

Internet of things (IoT) is a rapidly expanding market that is expected to reach more than 500 billion US dollars by 2025.

IoT allows you to gather data from your various devices like sensors or manufacturing machines. There are over 10 billion active IoT devices worldwide.

IoT data is leveraged to drive business outcomes such as detecting production line failures, improving parcel traceability, and fleet monitoring.

Data Integration is implemented to collect data from IoT devices and feed it to business applications that will deploy and derive value from these use cases.

Let's take an example from Smart Electronics. Smart Electronics has upgraded its production line with new sensors to compute various metrics like temperature, humidity, and line speed.

Smart Electronics would like to identify "risky" situations, such as a high temperature on the line or an abnormal speed, in order to prevent production disruptions and failures.

The Data Integration layer will gather data from the IoT devices and sensors and send them to a centralized web and mobile application monitored by the factory management with alert notifications pushed in the case of abnormal situations.

Conclusion

Data Integration is a critical capability within information systems.

Data Integration provides a large set of benefits, such as reducing time to market, avoiding costs associated with poor data quality or manual data transfer, and improving the customer journey.

Data Integration enables the integration of disparate and heterogeneous systems and provides a connectivity layer to a variety of applications and offers orchestration capabilities to automate business processes and transform data.

Data Integration can be implemented using various patterns like ETL, ESB, EDI or Data Virtualizations to meet different needs and reach business objectives.

Data Integration can aid in the development of a highly available solution for data exchange by utilizing the appropriate technical architecture. It also helps in securing data exchange through authentication and encryption mechanisms, ensuring data confidentiality and integrity.

The selection of a data integration solution is a structuring decision for the information system, and a rigorous process should be followed to choose, test and implement the data integration layer, as suggested by the DIPF.

Once implemented, a data integration layer will emerge and should be supported by the appropriate operations management model and processes.

In the coming years, data Integration will continue to drive high talent demand in the market, with new trends of enhancing its capabilities through integrations with other digital tools and applied artificial intelligence, as well as enabling digital transformation and a wide range of use cases in IoT, Predictive and Data Science.

Bonus

As a thank you for purchasing this book, I am offering you unlimited and free access to my course on Udemy, Data Integration Guide. Please scan this QR Code to claim your free coupon,

If you have any questions or need assistance, feel free to contact me on LinkedIn! I will be more than happy to help. My LinkedIn profile is here: https://www.linkedin.com/in/ahmedfessi/

You can also subscribe to our newsletter, get updated materials and follow new publications and news by visiting: https://dataintegrationguide.com/

Dedication

To my daughter Donia,

To my mom Essia, to my dad Abdellatif,

To my wife Imen,

To my brother Aymen and my sister Anissa,

To all my teachers from elementary to university,

To all family, friends, colleagues, professionals, and industry
leaders who helped me learn and grow throughout my career.

Copyright © 2022

Ahmed Fessi

All rights reserved

Data Integration Guide

Notice of Copyright

Independently published

2022

First Printing Edition, 2022
ISBN 9798835074501

Printed in Great Britain
by Amazon

61170651R00117